CHILDREN

with

ADHD

From Diagnosis to Graduation

A STEP-BY-STEP GUIDE

Volume 1

REGAN HILTON

TABLE OF CONTENTS

INTRODUCTION

Is your child an "earthquake"? Doesn't he listen to you? Is he distracted? Does he do things halfway?

Do his teachers, your friends, his general practitioner point out to you that the child is particularly restless? Do they report at school that it could "be ADHD"?

Let's talk about it, don't despair!

ADHD, Attention Deficit / Hyperactivity Disorder, is an evolutionary disorder of self-control. It is a disorder connected with the personal difficulty of regulating one's behavior according to the time available, goals and requests. It is not the result of a wrong or insufficient education, nor of a premeditated opposition of the child to the demands of parents or school.

Otherwise, being "restless" does not necessarily mean "having ADHD" and restlessness can be due to multiple reasons.

According to doctors, as testified by Dr. Andreas Wechsler, pediatrician, too often the term "hyperactive" is used inappropriately: children who have a clinical picture attributable to an ADHD that has characterized them since early childhood, correspond to 5 %. In all other cases, it is a question of motor restlessness, a widespread phenomenon of various kinds but on which it is possible to intervene, starting from the lifestyle and an appropriate approach to the child, with sometimes surprising results.

It is therefore two very different things.

Restlessness is often considered an integral part of children's nature and seems to be part of their way of being, but in reality, it has external causes, for example environmental: some of these have been identified in the frenetic pace of today's society.

ADHD, on the other hand, is a neurodevelopmental disorder characterized by inattention, impulsivity and motor hyperactivity that makes it difficult and in some rare cases prevents the normal development, integration and social adaptation of children, adolescents and adults. In the face of the child's lack of behavioral self-control and the failure of various educational and disciplinary measures, in the face of the great stress and frustration that both parents, teachers, and children experience, a request for help to the pediatrician is generally reached.

How is the diagnosis reached?

The first step in diagnosing it is in fact up to the pediatrician, who subjects the child to a thorough check in order to exclude other pathologies.

Only at a later stage, if the doctor deems it necessary, can you go to a specialist to whom all aspects of family and school life that appear in some way connected to the child's behavior must be reported by parents and teachers.

There are no diagnostic tests capable of exhaustively investigating all the nuances of the disorder, it is a diagnosis that requires the use of multiple sources.

The main tools available to the specialist to diagnose ADHD are: questionnaires, interviews, structured observation, cognitive and neuropsychological tests.

What to do on a daily basis if diagnosed with ADHD?

The following are some simple but fundamental tips to lighten everyday life and help the child to live better with their disorder.

Communicate in a linear fashion, making one request at a time, making sure it is fulfilled.

It is essential that in the family you get used to talking to the child by expressing, in a few words, one thought at a time, in a gentle and firm way. E.g: "Roberto, as soon as you come back from school you will tidy your room, please". It is not appropriate to use phrases such as: "Let's see if you can tidy your room later, without making a fuss."

Daily routine

It is important for children to have a daily routine in which the rhythms are known; when this is not possible, it is advisable to provide a list of the day's commitments / activities. This will help them to predict the required attention or effort times and to dose the efforts, thus better facing the different daily difficulties.

Be a positive example

For children with ADHD, more than for many others, it is important to "see" how they should behave: having an example to imitate reassures them.

In order to establish an educational understanding with the adult, it would be advisable to ignore the slightly negative attitudes and punish only the very negative ones by depriving the child of something particularly pleasing to him, or forcing him to remain still for a few minutes to reflect on his attitude.

Reward and gratify positive behaviors

Getting an immediate reward for the willingness and commitment shown, not just for the result, will certainly induce the child to repeat the positive behavior.

Do not intervene in the acute phase

Never argue or seek agreement in the acute phase of the conflict. Allowing the child to "vent" when he is angry or stubbornly opposes requests is the only option. In quarrels between siblings, for example, it is appropriate to separate them and firmly reaffirm to let it go. If this is not enough then it will be necessary to impose TIME OUT with a clear signal. Once the quarrel has been settled, there is no need to immediately re-elaborate what happened but to resume the normal course of the day and return to the subject only later.

Replace "sermons" with contact

In ADHD it is good to replace verbal corrections: "I would like you now for a while to ...", "In my opinion now you should ..." with physical contact, for example a gentle pat on the back, a physical approach and a concrete indication how to do it ...

Floor time

Floor time is to carve out a special time of the day to be with their children for the pleasure of play. It is a time when you can do what the little one wants, participating in his game without taking control while being involved in it. The privileged interaction between adult and child, the soft element (a carpet), the floor and some toys create a rewarding educational context for both.

ADHD treatment is the result of teamwork between psychologists, pedagogists, psychotherapists, teachers and parents who help the child to become aware of his or her social difficulties and to "learn" those behaviors that allow him to access the reality that surrounds him more adequately.

The success of the intervention depends on the involvement of people who have an active role in the child's life. In this sense, the family is an essential resource to encourage the emergence of positive behaviors. However, the protective instinct of the parents and the availability towards the child are not sufficient to modify their behavior.

Recent studies have also demonstrated the validity of Parent Training, as a tool to support parents in raising their child. It is a path divided into a series of meetings in which specialized personnel work alongside the family to support them in dealing with situations of discomfort and in introducing the strategies indicated above, often not easy to apply when you are stressed and emotionally tried by a complex situation such as your child's disturbance. So, to help your child to live their condition in a serene way, it is necessary to build a village, a social network on which you and he can count to overcome moments of crisis.

Having a child with adhd syndrome creates family problems, feelings of guilt and paroxysmal anxiety for the future, but controlling this disorder with both drug and psychological therapies and with constant discipline that requires everyone's effort is possible. Having a child with adhd syndrome destabilizes you, but always remember that it is not your fault and that your child is not just the syndrome that they have been diagnosed with. Your son has a thousand facets ... he has limitations, like all human beings. The disease, the diagnosis, starts first

WHAT IS ADHD

ADHD Attention Deficit Hyperactivity Disorder

ADHD is characterized by disabling levels of inattention, disorganization and / or hyperactivity-impulsivity. It is estimated that 5% of children are affected.

ADHD (Attention Deficit Hyperactive Disorder) falls into the category of Neurodevelopmental Disorders, a group of conditions that begin in the period of development and are characterized by a deficit that causes impairment in personal, social, school or work functioning. Neurodevelopmental Disorders very often occur concurrently.

ADHD is characterized by disabling levels of inattention, disorganization and / or hyperactivity-impulsivity. In the childhood bracket, ADHD often overlaps with disorders such as Oppositional-Provocative Disorder and Conduct Disorder. Moreover, it often persists into adulthood, causing impairment of functioning in the social, school and work spheres.

The presence of ADHD is estimated in about 5% of children and 2.5% of adults.

ADHD Diagnosis

The fundamental characteristic of ADHD is the persistent presence of a picture characterized by inattention and / or hyperactivity-impulsivity that interferes with development and functioning.

Inattention is highlighted, on the behavioral level, with diversion from the task, lack of perseverance, difficulty in maintaining attention, disorganization not attributable to attitudes of challenge or lack of understanding.

Hyperactivity implies excessive motor activity, squirming, the feeling that the child is "under pressure", drumming, talkativeness; such behaviors manifest themselves in moments and situations in which they are not appropriate. In adults, hyperactivity can express itself with extreme restlessness or the wearing effect on others of one's activity.

Impulsivity manifests itself in extremely hasty and instant actions, often with high risk for the individual. Impulsivity can express a desire for immediate reward, also manifesting itself in intrusive behaviors, such as interrupting others excessively, or making important decisions without reflecting on the possible long-term consequences.

Behavioral manifestations must occur in more than one context, such as home, school, work. It should also be considered that the symptoms of ADHD can vary depending on the specific context.

There are three sub-types of the disorder:

Combined manifestation: most typical manifestation in developmental age, characterized by a combined picture of symptoms of inattention and hyperactivity-impulsivity.

Manifestation with predominant inattention: the symptoms are mainly detectable in the "inattention" category compared to the "hyperactivity-impulsivity" category. Children belonging to this subtype of disorder have fewer behavioral problems and fewer difficulties in interactions with peers; this can lead parents and teachers to neglect the symptoms. They may sit quietly, but their attention is not directed at what they are doing or what the teacher is explaining.

Manifestation with predominant hyperactivity-impulsivity: most of the symptoms are highlighted in the "hyperactivity-impulsivity" category. Few symptoms of inattention may be present, but they do not reach a threshold of clinical relevance.

Onset and course of ADHD

ADHD onset in childhood. There is no specification of an age of onset. It is frequently identified during the elementary school years, where even inattention is more disabling. The symptomatological picture is more stable in early adolescence, in some cases, however, there may be a worsening, with the appearance of antisocial behaviors.

In the pre- school age, hyperactivity is prominently highlighted, while in the primary school age group, inattention emerges more. In the adolescent phase, the signs of hyperactivity occur less frequently, mainly characterized only by agitation, a more internal feeling of nervousness, restlessness or impatience. In adulthood, impulsiveness, together with Inattention and restlessness, can remain at problematic levels, even though hyperactivity has decreased.

Causes of ADHD

The research has highlighted the important role played by genetic factors on the development of ADHD. Genetic transmission affects the levels of motor activity, therefore a hereditary basis for the disorder is hypothesized. It has been shown that the weight of genetic factors on the development of the disorder is greater in the presence of symptoms of greater severity.

Different neurobiological characteristics have been found in the presence of ADHD that result in a deficit in inhibitory behavior, emotional regulation, maintenance of attention levels and in the processes of planning and execution of motor responses.

In the etiology of ADHD, we must also consider the biological variables that occur in the pre or perinatal period and which may involve brain damage or particular difficulties related to the course of pregnancy, childbirth, or which may occur in early childhood.

Another important role is that played by the conflictual interactions that are established between parents and child, which would influence by considerably increasing the probability that the disorder manifests itself in full, in all its severity.

Psychopathological Constructs of ADHD

The neurological deficit identifiable in the disorder seems to become the basis on which the behavioral aspects that characterize ADHD are grafted. It is precisely these behaviors that become protagonists of reactions and chain effects that invest the world of the child's relationships and his perception of himself. It happens extremely frequently that in mothers of children with ADHD, controlling behaviors towards the child develop mainly centered on the use of excessive and incoherent reprimands that prove to be ineffective. The alternation between parental behaviors marked by tight control and the renunciation of managing the child's behaviors determine a maintenance circuit which, in turn, influences as a factor that maintains or further decreases the child's self-esteem. These behaviors, which are often accompanied by those present in the other contexts of the child's life, such as the school in which isolation from peers is frequent as a result, reinforce a negative view of self, which maintains and strengthens symptomatic behaviors.

ADHD Treatment

The treatment of ADHD involves a multimodal intervention capable of combining pharmacological, psycho-educational and psychotherapeutic interventions.

Psychostimulants are believed to be the most effective drugs for adolescents, children and adults with ADHD. Among the drugs used are the methylphenidate (Ritalin), amphetamines (Adderal), the destoanfetamine (Dextrostat, Dexedrine) and the atomoxetine (Strattera). The main positive effects are borne by maintaining attention levels, impulsivity and hyperactivity.

In order for there to be lasting improvements over time, it is essential to combine pharmacological treatment with a combined path of cognitive and behavioral strategies that help children, parents and teachers to reach a full understanding of the problem and in the management of the problematic behaviors present.

The cognitive-behavioral programs of proven efficacy for ADHD foresee various levels of interlinked intervention that involve: the family, the school environment, the individual treatment of the child.

ADHD in the family: intervention with parents

The intervention programs directed at parents (ADHD Parent Training) aim to increase awareness and knowledge of the ADHD disorder, developing management skills on the part of parents and modifying the dysfunctional behaviors implemented in the relationship with the child. The main focus of the intervention is placed on the development of greater reflexive skills by parents, to help them acquire greater coherence and stability in their educational strategies that help and support the child in acquiring the ability to self-manage. A fundamental role is played by promoting a better emotional climate in the family and a more effective communication with the child, also by defining better limits and rules to follow.

ADHD at school: intervention with teachers

The intervention addressed to teachers (ADHD Teacher Training) has the aim of providing in a first phase the information necessary to achieve a full knowledge of ADHD. This constitutes an important prerequisite for a recognition of the positive aspects of the child to be initiated. It becomes central in this perspective to provide teachers with information on a structuring of the school environment that takes into account the needs and characteristics of the hyperactive child, to enhance his attention skills and learning. In addition, teachers should be provided with useful strategies for managing and modifying dysfunctional behaviors, as well as improving their relationships with peers.

Intervention with the child

Cognitive-behavioral therapy with the child with ADHD is addressed synergistically to all areas involved in the disorder and deficiency. The child is taught strategies that guide him in a systematic way in planning his own behavior in different areas of life and in solving problems (Problem Solving). Great attention is paid to the acquisition of the ability to monitor one's actions, developing a capacity for self-regulation towards impulsiveness and inattention. The child also learns to draw important information from their mistakes to correct themselves, but also to know how to reward themselves for achieving positive results. The intervention is also aimed at increasing social skills, through compliance with the rules, the development of more effective interactions and the ability to decode the emotional state of others, in order to respond and relate in an adequate and functional way. When ADHD is diagnosed, many parents feel hopelessly lost, and shame, guilt, frustration, all feelings that worsen the family environment and the course of their child's disorder, go into crisis. Each of us would always want the best for their child, but living with this disorder is possible, even if tiring. In this book we will try to give you practical advice for everyday life, so that your child can live in a more peaceful way both at home and at school. Don't feel alone you are not the only ones in this situation: seek help, arm yourself with a lot of patience, adopt a behavioral strategy together with teachers and psychologists and you will see that with your love, one day at a time, you will obtain small successes, which will improve the quality of life for you and your child.

THE DISORDER, THE SYMPTOMATOLOGY

Attention Deficit / Hyperactivity Disorder is considered a neurodevelopmental disorder. Neurological development disorders are neurological conditions that appear in early childhood, usually before entering school, and impair the development of personal, social, academic and / or occupational functioning basis. They generally include difficulties with acquiring, maintaining, or applying specific skills or sets of information. Neurodevelopmental disorders can involve alterations in one or more of one of the following aspects: attention, memory, perception, language or social relationships. Other frequent neurodevelopmental disorders include autism spectrum disorders, learning disorders (eg, dyslexia), and intellectual disability. Some experts have previously considered attention deficit / hyperactivity disorder a behavior disorder, likely because children generally exhibit inattentive, impulsive, and hyperactive behavior, and because the comorbidity of behavioral disorders, particularly oppositional defiant disorder and conduct disorder, are frequent. However, attention deficit / hyperactivity disorder has a well-established neurological basis and is not simply "misbehavior".

The percentage of school-age children affected by attention deficit / hyperactivity disorder is between 8 and 11 %. However, attention deficit / hyperactivity disorder is believed to be overdiagnosed due to imprecise use of clinical criteria. According to the Diagnostic and Statistical Manual of Mental Disorders, Fifth Edition (DSM-5), there are 3 types:

- Variant with predominant inattention
- Variant with predominant hyperactivity / impulsivity
- Combined

Overall, attention deficit / hyperactivity disorder is about twice as common in males, although relationships vary by type. The predominantly hyperactive / impulsive variant occurs 2 to 9 times more frequently in males; the predominantly inattentive type occurs with similar frequency in both sexes. Attention deficit / hyperactivity disorder tends to recur within the same family.

Attention Deficit / Hyperactivity Disorder does not recognize a single specific cause. The possible causes of attention deficit / hyperactivity disorder are represented by genetic, biochemical, sensory-motor development, physical as well as environmental-behavioral components. Risk factors are recognized birth weight <1500 g, head injury, iron deficiency, obstructive sleep apnea, lead exposure, and prenatal exposure to alcohol, tobacco, and cocaine. Just under 5% of children with attention deficit / hyperactivity disorder have evidence of neurological damage. Increasing evidence points to the involvement of dopaminergic and noradrenergic neurotransmitters, in particular due to a reduced activity of the upper part of the brain stem and of the fronto- mesencephalic connections.

Attention Deficit / Hyperactivity Disorder in Adults

Although attention deficit / hyperactivity disorder is considered a disorder of children and always begins in childhood, the underlying neurophysiological differences persist into adult life, and behavioral symptoms continue to be evident in adulthood in about half of cases. Although the diagnosis may occasionally not be recognized until adolescence or adulthood, some manifestations must have occurred before age 12.

In adults, symptoms include

- ✓ Difficulty concentrating
- ✓ Difficulty completing tasks (problems with executive functions)
- ✓ Mood swings
- ✓ Impatience
- ✓ Difficulty in maintaining relationships

Hyperactivity in adults usually manifests itself as continual restlessness and agitation rather than the overt motor hyperactivity that occurs in young children. Adults with attention deficit / hyperactivity disorder tend to be at higher risk of unemployment, reduced academic achievement, and increased rates of substance abuse and crime. Motor vehicle accidents and violations are more frequent.

Attention deficit / hyperactivity disorder may be more difficult to diagnose during adulthood. Symptoms can be similar to those of mood disorders, anxiety disorders, and substance use disorders. Because self-reports of childhood symptoms can be unreliable, doctors may need to review school records or ask family members questions to confirm manifestations before age 12.

Adults with attention deficit / hyperactivity disorder may benefit from the same type of stimulant medications as children with attention deficit / hyperactivity disorder. They may also benefit from counseling to improve time management and other management skills.

Symptomatology

The onset of symptoms often occurs in the first 4 years of age and in any case always before the age of 12. The age at which the diagnosis is generally made is between 8 and 10 years; however, individuals belonging to the inattentive variant may not be diagnosed until after adolescence.

The main symptomatology of attention deficit / hyperactivity disorder is represented by

- ✓ Inattention
- ✓ Impulsiveness
- ✓ Hyperactivity

Inattention is manifested when the child is involved in tasks that require concentration, rapid reaction times, capacity for selective visual and perceptive attention, for overall and selective listening for a prolonged time.

Impulsivity refers to hasty actions that have the potential for a negative outcome (eg, in children, who cross a street without looking, in teens and adults, who suddenly drop out of school or leave a job without think about the consequences).

Hyperactivity involves excessive motor activity. Children, particularly younger ones, may have difficulty sitting quietly when they should (eg, at school or church). Older patients may simply be restless, agitated, or talkative, sometimes to the point that others feel exhausted just looking at them.

Inattention and impulsiveness prevent the development of normal school skills and thinking and reasoning strategies; they demotivate school learning and create difficulties in adapting to social demands. Children with variant attention deficit / hyperactivity disorder with predominant inattention are subjects who learn by verbal transmission; have learning difficulties that require self-regulation in the performance of tasks and the use of organizational strategies to complete a task.

A specific learning disorder is associated in 20-60% of children with attention deficit / hyperactivity disorder, but some academic difficulty is present in the majority of children with attention deficit / hyperactivity disorder (hence missing details derive) and impulsiveness (hence answering questions without reflecting).

Behavioral history may reveal low frustration tolerance, oppositionality, temper tantrums, aggression, antisocial behavior and poor peer socialization, sleep disturbances, anxiety, dysphoria, depression, and mood swings.

Although there are no specific objective or laboratory signs associated with attention deficit / hyperactivity disorder, they may be present:

- ✓ Motor awkwardness or lack of coordination
- ✓ Non-localized nuanced neurological signs
- ✓ Perceptual-motor dysfunctions

Diagnosis

Clinical criteria based on DSM-5

Diagnosis of attention deficit / hyperactivity disorder is clinical and is based on comprehensive medical, developmental, educational, and psychological assessments (see also the American Academy of Pediatrics Clinical Practice Guideline for Diagnosis, Assessment, and Treatment of Deficit Disorder attention / hyperactivity in children and adolescents).

DSM-5 Criteria for Diagnosing Attention Deficit / Hyperactivity Disorder

DSM-5 diagnostic criteria include 9 symptoms and signs of inattention and 9 of hyperactivity and impulsivity. Diagnosis by these criteria requires $\geq$ 6 symptoms and signs from one or each group. Also, the symptoms have to:

- ✓ Be present often for $\geq$ 6 months
- ✓ Be much more evident than expected for a child of equal development
- ✓ Occur in at least 2 situations (eg, at home and at school)
- ✓ Be present before age 12 (at least some symptoms)
- ✓ Interfere with features at home, school, or work

Symptoms of inattention:

- ✓ Doesn't pay attention to detail or makes careless mistakes in schoolwork or other activities
- ✓ Has difficulty paying attention during homework or while playing
- ✓ He doesn't seem to listen when spoken to directly
- ✓ Has difficulty following instructions or fails to complete required tasks
- ✓ Has difficulty organizing tasks and activities
- ✓ Avoids, becomes uninterested in, or refuses to perform tasks that require sustained mental activity over a long period of time
- ✓ Often misses out on things needed for schoolwork or activities
- ✓ Is easily distracted

✓ Is careless in daily activities

Symptoms of hyperactivity and impulsivity:

✓ Often moves his hands or feet or cannot sit upright
✓ Gets up in class or in situations where he is expected to remain seated
✓ Runs around or climbs excessively when such activities are inappropriate
✓ Has difficulty playing quiet activities
✓ Moves continuously as if loaded by a spring
✓ Talks excessively
✓ Often answers even before the questions are completed
✓ Finds it hard to wait for his turn
✓ Often interrupts or behaves intrusively

Diagnosis of the predominant inattentive type requires ≥ 6 symptoms of inattention. Diagnosis of the hyperactive / impulsive type requires ≥ 6 symptoms and signs of hyperactivity and impulsivity. Diagnosis of the combined type requires ≥ 6 symptoms of inattention and hyperactivity / impulsivity.

Other Diagnostic Considerations

Differential diagnosis between attention deficit / hyperactivity disorder and other conditions can be difficult. To avoid diagnostic overestimation, other conditions must be properly evaluated and excluded. Many symptoms of attention deficit / hyperactivity disorder appearing in preschool can be related to communication problems present in other neurodevelopmental disorders (eg, autism spectrum disorders) or in some learning, anxiety, or mental disorders. depression or behavioral in nature (eg, conduct disorder).

Physicians must understand whether the child is inattentive due to problems reactive to external stimuli (ie, environmental inputs) or to internal problems (ie, thought disorder, anxiety, restlessness). During late childhood, however, signs of attention deficit / hyperactivity disorder become more easily identifiable; Children with the hyperactive-compulsive type or the combined type often have elevated motor activity levels with continuous limb movement (eg, non-purposeful hand and foot movement), impulsive speech, and a lack of awareness of possible environmental risks linked to their hyperactivity. Children belonging to the inattentive variant may have no physical symptoms.

Medical evaluation aims to identify potentially treatable conditions that contribute to or cause symptoms. Assessment should include looking for a history of prenatal exposures (eg, drugs, alcohol, tobacco), perinatal complications or infections, central nervous system infections, head trauma, heart disease, sleep breathing disorders, poor appetite, and / or squeamish eating, and a family history of attention deficit / hyperactivity disorder.

Developmental assessment serves to focus on the onset and course of symptoms. Assessment includes checking developmental milestones, particularly language milestones, and using specific rating scales for attention deficit / hyperactivity disorder. Versions of these scales are available for both families and school staff. , allowing for assessment in different situations as required by the DSM-5 criteria. Note that scales should not be used alone to make a diagnosis.

The analysis of the educational aspects allows to identify the essential symptoms; it is necessary to record the behavioral aspects through observation scales and compilation of checklists. However, observation scales and checklists individually do not allow distinguishing attention deficit / hyperactivity disorder from other developmental or behavioral disorders.

Prognosis

Beginning of school and interactions with the class group exacerbate the symptoms of children with attention deficit / hyperactivity disorder not yet diagnosed or inadequately treated. Difficulties in social and emotional relationships can persist during growth. Poor peer acceptance and social withdrawal tends to increase with age and with worsening of symptoms. Attention deficit / hyperactivity disorder when not identified and properly treated can lead to substance abuse, in fact, many adolescents and sick adults self-cure with legal (eg, caffeine) and illegal (eg, cocaine) substances.

Although symptoms lessen with age, adolescents and adults may continue to have other associated disorders. Predictors of negative prognosis in adolescence and adulthood are the presence of:

- ✓ Low intellectual level
- ✓ Aggression
- ✓ Social and interpersonal problems

Presence of psychopathology in the family

In adolescence and adulthood there are problems mainly related to school failure, low self-esteem and the ability to develop appropriate social behavior or not. Adolescents and adults with predominantly impulsive attention deficit / hyperactivity disorder may have a high incidence of personality disorders and antisocial behaviors; most of them continue to show impulsiveness, hyperactivity and difficulties in social relationships. Individuals with attention deficit / hyperactivity disorder seem to adapt better to work rather than study and home activities, particularly in work that does not require high levels of attention to perform.

Treatment - Behavioral therapy

Drug therapy with stimulant drugs such as methylphenidate or dextroamphetamine (in short- and long-acting preparations)

Randomized controlled trials show that behavioral therapies and drug therapy are less effective when used alone for school-aged children, but behavioral or combination therapy is recommended for younger children. Although drugs do not correct the underlying neurophysiological differences in patients with attention deficit / hyperactivity disorder, they are nevertheless effective in relieving symptoms and allow the patient to participate in activities and tasks previously impossible due to poor attention and impulsivity. Drugs allow you to control abnormal behaviors, thus enhancing cognitive behavioral interventions, motivation and self-esteem.

Treatment of attention deficit / hyperactivity disorder in adults follows similar rules, but the choice of drug and doses must be determined individually, taking into account any other associated pathologies.

Stimulant drugs

Psychostimulant drugs represented by methylphenidate or amphetamine salts are the most used. The response is variable and the dosage depends on the severity of the symptoms, behavior and individual tolerance of the drug. The dosage is changed in frequency and quantity until the optimal balance between response and adverse effects is achieved.

The methylphenidate is usually used beginning with 0.3 mg / kg orally 1 time / day (immediate release form), and increased in weekly frequency, typically from about 2 to 3 times / day or every 4 hours during the hours of wakefulness; many doctors try to use the morning and mid-day dosage. The dosage can be increased when the results are not satisfactory but the drug is still tolerated. Most children find an optimal balance between benefits and adverse effects at doses between 0.3 and 0.6 mg / kg. The dextrorotatory isomer of methylphenidate is half as active and is available for prescription for half the dose.

The dextroamphetamine is usually initiated (often in combination with racemic amphetamine) to 0.15 to 0.2 mg / kg orally 1 time / day, which can then be increased up to 2 or 3 times / day or every 4 h during the waking hours. Single doses between 0.15 and 0.4 mg / kg are usually effective. Dose titration must balance efficacy against adverse effects; actual doses vary significantly between individuals, but, in general, higher doses increase the likelihood of unacceptable adverse effects. In general, the posology of dextroamphetamine is approximately two thirds of that of methylphenidate.

For both methylphenidate and dextroamphetamine, once the optimal dosology has been identified, the extended-release formulation will be used at the same dose, in order to avoid the need to administer the drugs at school. The long- acting formulations are slow-release matrix wax tablets, biphasic capsules containing the equivalent of 2 doses, and osmotic-release pills and transdermal patches that allow coverage up to 12 h. Short and long-acting liquid preparations are now available. Pure dextroamphetamine preparations (eg, dextromethylphenidate) are often used to minimize adverse effects such as anxiety; they are usually given in doses of about half that of mixed preparations. Prodrug preparations are used because of their characteristics, namely slow release, longer duration of action, fewer adverse effects and lower abuse potential. Improved learning is achieved with low doses, while behavioral improvement often requires higher doses.

Stimulant drug dosing schedules may be adjusted to cover specific days and times (eg, school hours and homework). It is possible to try drug breaks especially during weekends, holidays, or during the summer holidays. The periods in which the placebo is administered (from 5 to 10 school days to be sure of the reliability of the observations) are indicated to assess the real need for the drug.

Common adverse effects of stimulant drugs include:

- ✓ Sleep disturbances (eg, insomnia)
- ✓ Depression
- ✓ Headache
- ✓ Gastralgia
- ✓ Decreased appetite
- ✓ Tachycardia and high blood pressure

Although not proven by consistent scientific evidence, some studies have shown a slowdown in growth over 2 years of use of stimulant drugs, and it remains unclear whether this slowdown persists even for longer periods of administration. Some patients who are particularly sensitive to the effects of the drug may experience hyperconcentration or numbness; in such cases it may be useful to reduce the doses or replace the stimulant drug.

Non-stimulant drugs

Atomoxetine, a selective norepinephrine reuptake inhibitor, is also used. The drug is effective, but the data on its effectiveness compared to stimulant drugs are conflicting. Some children have nausea, sedation, irritability and temper tantrums; severe liver toxicity and suicidal thoughts may occur rarely. The usual starting dose is 0.5 mg / kg orally once / day, increased to 1.2 to 1.4 mg / kg weekly. The long half-life allows once / day administration, although it requires continuous use to be effective. The maximum recommended daily dose is 100 mg.

Antidepressants such as bupropion, alpha-2 agonists such as clonidine and guanfacine, and other psychoactive drugs are sometimes used in cases of psychostimulants that are ineffective or have severe adverse effects, although they are less effective and are not recommended as first line medications. Sometimes these drugs are used in combination with stimulants for synergistic effects; close monitoring for adverse effects is essential.

Adverse drug interactions are of concern for the treatment of attention deficit / hyperactivity disorder. Drugs that inhibit the metabolic enzyme CYP2D6, including some selective serotonin reuptake inhibitors which are sometimes used in patients with attention deficit / hyperactivity disorder, may enhance the effect of stimulant drugs. Reviewing potential drug interactions (typically using a computer program) is an important part of the drug management of patients with attention deficit / hyperactivity disorder.

Behavioral therapy

Counseling, which includes cognitive-behavioral therapy (p. Eg., goal- setting, self-monitoring, modeling, imitation), is often effective and helps the child to understand the disorder of attention deficit / hyperactivity disorder and how to deal with it. Respect for the rules and routine are essential.

Behavior in the classroom is often improved by the reduction of noisy and visual environmental stimuli, by the administration of tasks of appropriate duration, by training and by the proximity of the teacher.

When difficulties persist at home, parents should be encouraged to seek professional assistance from specialists, and supported in the practice of managing behavioral techniques. Adding incentives and rewards helps with behavior management and is often effective. Once modus operandi and limits have been established and parents have well acquired management techniques, children are often better looked after at home, especially those with attention deficit / hyperactivity disorder in which hyperactivity and poor control prevail. of impulses.

The exclusion diets of some foods, vitamin supplements, antioxidants or other compounds, nutritional or biochemical interventions were less effective. Biofeedback may be useful in some cases, but is not routinely recommended as evidence of efficacy is lacking.

Key points

Attention deficit / hyperactivity disorder involves inattention, hyperactivity / impulsivity, or a combination; it typically appears before age 12, even in preschool children.

The cause is unknown, but there are a number of suspected risk factors.

Diagnosis is based on clinical criteria, and focus should also be on other disorders that may have a similar onset (eg, autistic-like disorders, learning or behavioral disorders, anxiety, depression).

Manifestations tend to decrease with age, but some difficulties may persist in adolescents and adults.

Dealing with stimulant medications and cognitive-behavioral therapy; behavior therapy may be appropriate for preschool children.

The diagnosis must be made by child psychologists or neuropsychiatrists who use the criteria indicated by the DSM-IV (the most important and widespread international diagnostic manual of psychiatry on mental disorders).

Experts must also carry out a personal medical history of the child and his / her family and carry out a careful observation of the child's behavior, also using special grids to evaluate his behavior more in depth.

The child's intellectual level should then be investigated using standardized and reliable tests, carefully examining various functions such as attention, memory, planning and organization skills and sensorineural integrity.

The child psychologist or neuropsychiatrist must carry out a very detailed interview with the child's parents on the type of behavior that the child adopts in different social contexts and on his ability to maintain concentration towards certain activities for a certain period of time (in carrying out homework and structured games, listening to a story, etc.).

Parents and teachers of the child may also be asked to fill in a questionnaire to assess the subject's behavior, also investigating his or her emotional sphere and the possible presence of problems in this area.

The symptoms of ADHD are most noticeable in situations that require a high level of attention and concentration or that are not new to the child (for example, when he has to take long lessons from teachers, has to do repetitive and not very fun activities, has to read long stories, etc.). These symptoms are especially evident in very noisy social contexts of an extended group (group games, etc.). Symptoms, on the other hand, are less evident when the child is facing an interesting and rewarding situation, in a context of a two-person relationship (for example when he is alone with the teacher or with the parent) especially if the relationship is positive for him. The person making the diagnosis (child psychologist or neuropsychiatrist) should therefore analyze the child's behavior in different contexts of his life (family, school, social, etc.) and in contexts of relationship in two, small or large group etc.

Finally, it must be pointed out that, to make a diagnosis of ADHD, the child's symptoms must be present in several areas and must not be exclusively found in a particular situation (for example only at school or in the family).

Risk elements for a child suffering from attention disorder with hyperactivity are:

- ✓ presence of aggression
- ✓ low level of intelligence
- ✓ negative relationships with peers
- ✓ persistence of symptoms in adolescence and adulthood.

The characteristics of attention deficit hyperactivity disorder are:

- ✓ inattention: the inability to remain attentive for some time on a stimulus continuously
- ✓ hyperactivity: the inability to stay still
- ✓ impulsiveness: the inability to evaluate the consequences of one's actions with the danger of running into dangerous situations.

Inattention can manifest itself with:

- ✓ difficulty paying attention especially to details making careless mistakes
- ✓ difficulty staying on the task without constantly switching from one activity to another and not completing one
- ✓ difficulty in carrying out carefully ordered work
- ✓ difficulty completing homework
- ✓ difficulty listening to conversations
- ✓ difficulty following instructions
- ✓ difficulty in carrying out activities that require concentration and organizational skills
- ✓ difficulty in maintaining constant attention, avoiding paying attention to external stimuli of little importance
- ✓ difficulty following directions or rules of games or activities
- ✓ difficulty in remembering to perform certain actions
- ✓ difficulty in being tidy and not frequently losing objects or other material that the child has with him.

Hyperactivity can be manifested by:

- ✓ difficulty staying still in one's chair

- ✓ difficulty in remaining seated in situations that require it
- ✓ difficulty in maintaining a correct and adequate behavior with respect to the place in which he is (the child runs, jumps, fidgets in situations where he should feel comfortable)
- ✓ difficulty playing or carrying out recreational activities without making too much noise
- ✓ difficulty keeping quiet (talks constantly)
- ✓ difficulty in carrying out a task without getting up all the time (for example when having to do homework or watch television, etc.)
- ✓ difficulty in waiting for one's turn during the activities carried out (ball games, etc.).

Impulsiveness manifests itself with:

- ✓ difficulty in restraining one's reactions, giving the answers before the questions have been completed
- ✓ difficulty waiting for one's turn, often interrupting others
- ✓ difficulty in listening to the directives given to him
- ✓ difficulty in being respectful of the spaces of others, instead entering frequently in situations that do not concern him
- ✓ difficulty avoiding starting conversations when the time isn't right
- ✓ difficulty in managing one's own behavior by not taking into consideration the presence of others
- ✓ difficulty in not interrupting others excessively
- ✓ difficulty in assessing the dangerous consequences of one's actions.

It should be pointed out that in some children there is a picture in which impulsiveness predominates, in others inattention, in still others hyperactivity. The three symptoms usually occur together.

The symptoms listed above are often associated with difficulties in enduring frustrations, aggressive behavior, sudden outbursts of anger, low self-esteem, depressive feelings, high level of anxiety, problems in conduct, inability to deal with one's own difficulties, low motivation.

These children are continually reprimanded for their disturbing behavior in the classroom and often achieve poor school results, thus increasing their experience of insecurity and inability. Often children with ADHD do not get successes and positive considerations even in sports or in the performance of other disciplines due to their restless and agitated conduct and their inability to follow established rules.

HOW TO RECOGNIZE THE ALARM BELLS

Often regulating one's behavior and orienting it according to one's needs and those of the surrounding environment is not as simple as it appears. In fact, there are children who show fatigue in organizing their daily activities, who do not listen to instructions and do not obey parents and teachers, engaging in impulsive and sometimes dangerous behaviors for themselves or for others. These are children suffering from Attention Deficit Hyperactivity Disorder which manifests itself with persistent symptoms of inattention, hyperactivity and / or impulsivity. However, it is not always easy to distinguish very lively and restless children from children who instead have a disease of clinical relevance, so where to start? In this chapter, we will look at what the red flags are for ADHD.

Let's try to clarify!

What are the risk factors in the onset of ADHD?

We can certainly refer to some risk factors that help us to establish a clearer clinical picture, among these we report some temperamental traits such as poor inhibition or the search for novelty, environmental factors such as low birth weight, smoking / alcohol in pregnancy, food intolerances, neglect etc. and genetic factors such as a history of ADHD, motor impairment, nutritional deficiencies or epilepsy.

What are the possible "red flags" of ADHD?

In addition to these risk factors, it is necessary to pay attention to some signals that can be activated already starting from kindergarten and that can guide us towards an early detection of the disorder. In preschool age, for example, we make particular reference to hyperactivity that manifests itself with attitudes such as the unstoppable need to move, which makes it difficult to establish contacts with others, , the inability to stay still, not being able to accept preordained rules and the excitement for new activities, which disappears after a few minutes and leads to repeatedly changing activities in progress.

During school age, on the other hand, inattention emerges more characterized by difficulties in planning sequential steps for the execution of particular activities, with consequent dispersion in school tasks, by the presence of distraction errors, by the inability to complete tasks, from disorganization and forgetfulness in respecting certain tasks, in addition to hasty tasks and the lack of self-correction.

Inattention is evident in those children who lose or forget personal items and who seem not to listen when asked for something.

Over the years, the symptoms of hyperactivity decrease, but the problems related to inattention remain and those related to impulsivity are added, which manifests itself with the effort to wait for one's turn and manage expectations, talking over peers or making irrelevant interruptions and with difficulty in predicting the consequences of their behavior, with consequent negative repercussions in the construction of their social relationships.

Why intervene early?

In general, it is necessary to intervene suddenly when these behaviors negatively affect the daily functioning of the child, within various contexts (for example both at home and at school).

An early treatment helps to monitor the symptoms so as to make the child more aware of his own functioning and able to learn more easily both the school constructs and the appropriate behavior patterns, moreover in this way his social relationships will also improve. it will reduce the risk of developing associated ailments and ensure a better future for the child.

DIAGNOSIS

We all probably know at least one hyperactive child. These children often behave very impulsively and act before they think. They have a hard time concentrating on one activity and often move from one thing to another randomly, without finishing the projects they start. Many of these children do not do the thing they were asked to do for more than a minute if it requires attention and effort over a long period. They seem to have an extraordinarily high energy level. Socially they stand out and demand attention, feelings and gratification.

Mothers of hyperactive children usually experience tremendous helplessness because their children have difficulty remembering that they shouldn't put their dirty hands on the walls when running from room to room; schoolmates complain that he spontaneously changes the rules of the game; his teacher finds himself in the situation where the child asks what to do immediately after detailed instructions are given to the whole class. He usually makes strange noises or sounds that annoy those around him. He constantly messes around, knocking his glass off the table, tripping over cables while chasing the dog, or dropping a model of a boat his grandfather had been building for months. Even if his intentions are good, his actions often annoy others and provoke rejection from those around him.

Hyperactivity is also referred to as infantile hyperkinesia and is a neurobiological disorder involving genetic and environmental factors. Hyperactivity is not a form of excessive vivacity or characteristic of a turbulent child, but a real disorder of the pre -frontal cortex and other subcortical structures involving motor activity area, and responsible to symptomatic and precise criteria.

The diagnosis of hyperactivity should always be evaluated with a specialist who can evaluate symptoms and therapy. We will see in detail the specific symptoms of infantile hyperkinesia a little later, but we can already anticipate some signs of hyperactivity in children in general:

Inability to stay still, hands and feet are always in motion.

Extreme liveliness and activity (running, climbing, etc)

Inability to focus on a single activity, you move from one activity to another without completing the first

Difficulty playing quiet games.

They are easily distracted

They have a hard time listening and following the instructions they are given

They talk a lot and don't listen.

They answer and interrupt each other's conversations.

They do not wait their turn in games or conversations and often participate in an impetuous form.

They do not perceive the sense of danger and very often do dangerous things without thinking about it.

They lose or forget what they have to do or what is needed to finish a task

As we can see, the main problem concerns the phenomenon of self-regulation which is expressed through behavioral forms but which involves different cognitive spheres (from the capacity of organization to executive functions, but also the mental representation of a goal or the inhibition of adequate responses to the situation.) In addition, this disorder also creates major relational problems for the child both towards parents, and towards other children or teachers, making it very often that the child is either not understood, or isolated or unable to make himself / herself to understand. Very often these relational disabilities lead the child to develop other disorders or tics as well, such as forms of anxiety and depression, learning delays and language difficulties.

Hyperactivity is usually diagnosed in the context of attention deficit hyperactivity disorder which is commonly referred to as ADHD syndrome. You have to specify in this case that the label ADHD belongs to the Association of American psychiatrists, while the World Health Organization speaks of hyperkinetic syndrome which is divided into hyperkinetic syndrome of conduct and disturbance of activity and attention .. The ADHD syndrome is defined, as we have seen, a disorder related to self-control, which is characterized by an inability to maintain attention for a prolonged period of time, a marked impulsivity and hyperactivity. This disorder is expressed in the behavioral sphere as the child is unable to regulate his behavior adequately according to the time or environment or the required and appropriate objectives.

Lack of attention and ADHD

We have seen that attention deficit along with impulsivity and hyperactivity is one of the components of ADHD. Normally in preschool age this disorder is characterized by the hyperactivity phase, while in the school age the first problems related to lack of attention are identified.

In any case, this attention deficit does not have to do with an intellectual disability, indeed hyperactive children tend to have above average intelligence, but are more sensitive than others to the stimuli they receive and thus process a greater range of information or tasks that they fail to complete.

Let's take a closer look at the symptoms of ADHD and what are the criteria on which the diagnosis is based.

Symptoms

Symptoms must appear before age 7 and be present for a minimum of 6 months to diagnose ADHD. At least 8 of the following 14 behaviors must be observed "more frequently than most people of the same mental age":

Frequent agitation that is demonstrated with hand and foot movements or while sitting

Difficulty sitting when the situation requires it;

Easy distraction due to external stimuli to the situation;

Difficulty keeping turns in games or group situations;

Hurried answers before the question ends;

Difficulty following the instructions of others (not due to a lack of understanding);

Difficulty maintaining attention during playful tasks or activities;

Frequent switching from one incomplete activity to another;

Difficulty playing quietly;

Often talks excessively;

Often interrupts or introduces himself into the activities of other children;

Often, he does not listen to what he is told;

Often loses things needed for a school task or activity;

Often engages in dangerous physical activities without evaluating the possible risks and not to seek strong emotions (for example, crossing a busy road without looking).

If you suspect that your child is hyperactive and / or that it coincides with the profile we have described, it is important to consult an Adhd specialist for a professional diagnosis and, if necessary, to start treatment as soon as possible.

Lively or hyperactive child?

How to distinguish a lively child from a hyperactive one? We have seen that the diagnosis of hyperactivity or ADHD syndrome takes a long time and the presence of different symptoms related to the three spheres of attention deficit, impulsivity and hyperactivity. Children love to move, jump and never sit still: a diagnosis cannot be based on simplistic terms and drugs must be given after an accurate diagnosis. It is important to evaluate the child's symptoms clearly and over time and with a qualified medical staff. Therefore, if you have any doubts, contact a specialist as soon as possible to evaluate the problem together.

Can we talk about a hyperactive newborn? Or can it be hyperactive 2-year-olds? 3?

We have seen that the diagnosis of hyperactivity is made starting from the seventh year of age, therefore in this age the first symptoms could be perceived, but the diagnosis will be made later.

It is true that the factors can be genetic, so in the case of hyperactivity in the family, you can think of turning to a specialist and expose your problem. Similarly, if you see that a newborn has sleep problems and is always active, or a 3-year-old child speaks and does not listen or does not respond correctly to environmental stimuli, you might consider seeking a specialist.

There are many causes that can lead young children into different behaviors. For example, the infant's sleep pattern may depend on several factors, including the infant's character or the relationship with the parents, not necessarily a hyperactivity disorder. Likewise, interaction with the environment can cause minor traumas that can affect different behaviors in many children. For any doubt or question it is always better to contact your pediatrician or a child psychologist so that he can accompany you towards the correct diagnosis of the problem.

How to calm a hyperactive child?

To calm a hyperactive child, it is important to have a lot of patience and try to avoid scolding and scolding, but play on positivity and assertiveness. In addition to these two points, you can try to favor a quiet and calm environment, avoiding activities that can agitate them and creating a peaceful atmosphere, starting with an attitude that must be calm and as serene as possible. This means trying to take the child to places that are not over-stimulating or not suddenly changing the plans of the day.

You need to create simple rules that the child is able to respect and at the same time organize the day to make is that the child does not get lost among other activities.

Games for hyperactive children

A good way to calm a hyperactive child is to offer him a game. As we have mentioned, it is better to avoid proposing all those activities that can agitate him even more (racing, contact or noisy games, etc) but it is better to propose also social games but to be done seated and calmly.

In addition, there are games that can help improve planning, self-control, attention and cognitive flexibility. They can be games connected to do-it- yourself, or games to be made in groups but with specific game rules to be respected: like steal the flag, or 1-2-3 star, in which you can only move if called or while the other it's counting and then you have to learn to stand still.

Other games such as Shanghai or Memory can also help train some cognitive and motor skills. The games played in the company, will allow the child to have fun and develop his social skills, improving his self-esteem and self-efficacy.

What to do if our child is hyperactive?

Relating to a hyperactive child is not easy, because if on the one hand his attitudes can lead to losing patience, on the other it must be considered that we are faced with a discomfort and that normal reproaches or educational forms could generate the opposite effect to what we want. What can we do in the family and at school to improve the relationship and communication with hyperactive children?

How to behave in the family

The parent training becomes a critical tool to understand how to behave in the family and to learn the best techniques to relate with their child. For example, we have already seen that repeatedly scolding the child for their wrong behaviors may not make sense, since it would make them feel even more insecure and lead to further isolation. In these cases, it could work on assertiveness and clarity, asking him one thing at a time through simple rules that the child can understand and that can help him achieve his goal, even through models of reward or denial to which they can easily associate a cause and effect for their actions. In any case, following specific training for families with hyperactive children can help improve the relationship and behavior of the child.

What to do at school

For hyperactive children, school is a predominantly negative place where they are forced to sit still and concentrate most of the time, two activities that can be very tiring and difficult for them. In this sense, teachers should also be able to adapt homework and different projects as much as possible to these children without making them feel different from the rest of the class. Obviously not being an easy task, teachers should be able to ask for help from parents who have already trained in parental training sessions or a specialist, to be able to build together a training method that helps the child in learning and social relations with the class.

ADHD MYTHS: THE CHILD IS JUST TOO LIVELY!

Sometimes the ADHD disorder is presented ideologically, thus addressing in an absolutely incorrect and misleading way the very delicate issue of Attention Deficit and Hyperactivity Disorder, creating confusion in parents and workers. In this chapter we dispel some clichés, myths, prejudices and serious inaccuracies on a scientific and social level that are sometimes heard and that cause serious damage not only to the scientific truth but above all to children and adolescents with ADHD and their families.

ADHD IS NOT SIMPLE VIVACITY ...

ADHD with its varied picture of associated disorders is not the simple liveliness or distraction which is typical in children but a real disorder that prevents those affected by it from selecting environmental stimuli, planning their actions and controlling their own impulses.

We parents, precisely through a road fraught with daily difficulties and sufferings, can testify that this disorder really puts our families, parents, schools, society in crisis, but above all it lets our children suffer and relegates them to a world of marginalization.

ADHD has a huge social impact: family tragedies primarily due to diagnoses not made in the past, ineffective therapies and unnecessary psychotherapy that lasted for years, criminal and civil complaints against parents due to serious behavior of their children in the social sphere, adults with this disorder not treated in their past who often live with sometimes severe psychiatric situations, worsening of ADHD symptoms in adolescents with the addition of conduct disorders, depressive or anxious disorders over time, failed marriages due to the stress generated by the disorder, serious consequences induced in siblings and much more.

Attention Deficit Hyperactivity Disorder (ADHD) is one of the most frequent neuropsychiatric disorders with onset in developmental age, characterized by inattention, impulsivity and motor hyperactivity that compromises many stages of development and social integration of children. It is a heterogeneous and complex, multifactorial disorder that in 70-80% of cases coexists with another or other disorders (a phenomenon called comorbidity), a factor that aggravates the symptoms making both diagnosis and therapy complex. The most frequently associated are oppositional-defiant disorder and conduct disorders, specific learning disorders (dyslexia, dysgraphia, etc.), anxiety disorders and, less frequently, depression, obsessive-compulsive disorder, tic disorder, bipolar disorder.

ADHD is a chronic neurobiological disorder with the highest prevalence in school age but which tends to persist even into adolescence and adulthood in 50-60% of cases.

Through neuroimaging techniques (functional magnetic resonance and positron emission tomography) and molecular genetic studies it was possible to highlight that ADHD is really a disorder of biological origin of the pre- frontal cortex and of the basal nuclei that involves an alteration in the processing of responses to environmental stimuli and the ability to concentrate.

The last forty years of research of this disorder have led to the consideration and study of numerous factors at its origin (it is in fact a multifactorial disorder) and among these genetic factors (being a polygenic disorder with a heritability factor greater than

75 %, there are many candidate genes studied in the dopamine and norepinephrine neurotransmission system associated with important brain inhibition and modulation functions), cerebral morphological factors (frontal cortex, caudate nucleus and pale globe are smaller in ADHD children), prenatal and perinatal factors, traumatic factors. In this variegated complex of causes, it must always be considered that the activation of the predisposition to the disorder is probably also modulated by environmental factors (family, education, social contexts, etc.).

The diagnosis of ADHD is currently exclusively of the "clinical" type and is based on the classification of the Diagnostic Manual of Mental Disorders (DSM-IV) through an accurate assessment of the child conducted by specialists with specific skills relating to the diagnosis and therapy of ADHD and other disorders often present in comorbidities or in differential diagnoses. The assessment is extremely complex because it must involve not only the child but also his parents and teachers in order to collect information on the behavior and functional impairment of the child from multiple sources and in relation to multiple contexts. This analysis also includes the evaluation of cultural factors and the living environment in which the child is inserted, which makes use of tools such as questionnaires and semi-structured diagnostic interviews suitably standardized and validated.

The bibliography on ADHD is endless since it has been the most studied developmental psychiatric disorder for over a century and the field of studies and research worldwide covers all aspects of the disorder (assessment and diagnosis, classifications, aspects and courses of the disorder in adult life, epidemiological studies, comorbidities , etiology, pathophysiology, neurobiology) and treatment interventions (psychoeducational, psychosocial, behavioral therapy, improvement of social competence, pharmacological interventions with psychostimulants and pharmacological alternatives to psychostimulants), with over 7000 studies published in the most authoritative international scientific journals.

Despite this extraordinary mass of studies and clinical research, of a consolidated (but always perfectible) multidisciplinary diagnostic and multimodal therapeutic protocol, there are those who have doubts about the scientific reality of this disorder.

Well, it is necessary to underline, with the greatest possible force, how this position, characterized by gratuitous statements that do not refer to scientific studies or approaches, is in reality fraught with very harmful consequences. Among these, the denial of adequate treatment to those who would need it and that of dangerously misleading the layman as parents and teachers.

For this reason, some very clear and authoritative documents have been issued on this topic also because these doubts, amplified by the mass media, give the image of a divided scientific community on this aspect, while much more simply it must be considered that on the one hand there exist the real scholars and clinicians who study and face the challenge of ADHD in its actual reality and with scientific method and rigor and on the other "improvised workers" who believe they can approach the problem and clinical reality without a specific scientific preparation and an adequate cultural background, without a clinical practice and through the interpretation of old theories or misinterpretation of the same or even in purely ideological terms.

This situation is well described in the International Consensus Statement on ADHD of January 2002 (published in Clinical Child and Family Psychology Review , vol. 5, no. 2 June 2002) in which one of the most distinguished scholars, Prof. Russel Barkley, subscriber of the the same document together with 85 other prestigious ADHD scholars worldwide states: "The opinions of a handful of non-expert doctors who claim that ADHD does not exist are compared with established scientific opinions that claim otherwise, as if both views could enjoy equal merits. Such attempts ultimately give the public the feeling that there is substantial scientific disagreement as to whether ADHD is a real disorder. In fact, there is no such disagreement at all at least any more than there is on whether smoking can cause cancer or that the HIV virus causes AIDS. "

Some, however, want to promote in every way the scientific disavowal of the disorder with the main purpose of presenting in a scandalistic way the drug therapy which in reality represents, in the most serious cases, one of the approaches of the so-called "multimodal therapy". In fact, psychostimulants, in the most symptomatologically severe cases, are necessary and represent an important and decisive therapeutic resource, as is pointed out by all the world scientific literature of the last forty years and succinctly stated by Prof. Barkley in an article on it in Psychiatric Times : "The stimulant medications have demonstrated their efficacy in several hundred well-controlled scientific studies , making them not only one of the few success stories in child psychiatry of this century but the best - studied of any psychiatric (and other) medication prescribed for children "

MYTHS AND REALITY ABOUT THE DISORDER

Myth: ADHD is a sham disorder because it is diagnosed on the basis of symptoms and not on the basis of clinical diagnostic tests.

Reality: All neuropsychiatric disorders are diagnosed on the basis of symptoms and for none of them to date a specific clinical investigation is available that can detect them. There is no definitive clinical investigation to diagnose schizophrenia, autism, depression or bipolar disorder, but this does not mean that they can be denied. It should be noted, however, that for many years the progress of Neuroimaging techniques (Functional Magnetic Resonance - fMRI and Positron Emission Tomography-PET) have made it possible to highlight in children with ADHD a decrease in blood flow and / or oxygen consumption in the nuclei of the base and prefrontal cortex, precisely those brain areas that regulate attention, behavior programming, motor coordination and development and sense of time. These brain structures and the cerebellum in children with ADHD are also morphologically smaller (up to 6%) than in children in the "normal" reference group.

Myth: ADHD is a modern disorder born in the early 1980s when some psychiatrists claimed the existence of a new childhood mental illness.

Reality: It is known that the description of the disorder currently classified as ADHD dates back to the early 1900s with George Still and that the identification of the diagnostic category of Minimal Brain Dysfunction (MBD) dates back to the 1950s-1960s , with subsequent frequent changes in the definitions up to the current ADHD, DSM IV. The disorder is recognized as a real disability by all the major medical, psychiatric, psychological and educational associations worldwide.

Myth: ADHD is a disorder that regresses and disappears as the child grows.

Reality: ADHD is not only diagnosed in children. From the many follow-up studies conducted over the past decades it has now been shown that over 70% of children will continue to manifest the disorder in adolescence and about half in adulthood. If the disorder is not treated, individuals will tend to develop secondary problems such as depression, anxiety, substance abuse, existential failures in work and family life, antisocial conduct over the course of their life. Conversely, if the disorder is treated, most of the people affected will have a good emotional and productive life by managing the symptoms of the disorder fairly well.

Myth: ADHD is an environmental disorder due to poor parenting ability and lack of discipline.

Reality: The anachronistic idea is still widespread that the bad behavior of a child can be linked to a moral problem, that of the "bad" child. It has been unequivocally shown that working with greater discipline without any other intervention worsens rather than improves the behavior of children with ADHD. In reality, ADHD is a disorder that prevents those affected from selecting stimuli, planning actions and controlling impulses. All this because it is a chronic neurobiological disorder with numerous factors at its origin and among these genetic factors (genetic disorder with a heritability factor greater than 75%) cerebral morphological factors, prenatal and perinatal factors, traumatic factors. However, these factors do not exclude the fact that the activation of the predisposition of the disorder is modulated by "environmental" factors (family, education, social contexts, etc.) which, however, are not the cause.

Myth: ADHD is caused by too much sugar, preservatives and other artificial additives in food, and eliminating these substances from the diet can cure the disorder.

Reality: Studies have shown that very few children have benefited from special diets. Sugar and additives have been excluded from the causes of ADHD by dozens of "double-blind " studies (a double-blind clinical trial in which neither the participants nor the staff conducting the study know which participants are receiving the drug or trial object and such as a placebo).

TO GIVE MEDICINE OR NOT TO GIVE MEDICINE? THIS IS THE DILEMMA

Many sites and experts say that drug therapies should not be used to treat ADHD. Below we try to dispel some platitudes that circulate on the subject.

Myth: For a "paradoxical" effect contrary to what one would expect, by virtue of the particular metabolism of children these drugs numb children and keep them calm.

Reality: It is an absolutely false statement because the "paradoxical" effect occurs only on children affected by the disorder due to the typical mechanism of the drug that improves attention by reducing hyperactivity by modulating the amount of dopamine and noradrenaline in the synaptic space.

Myth: Stimulants can lead to addiction following prolonged treatment, as occurs with drugs.

Reality: Precisely because stimulants are able to promote concentration and consequently allow good school results by improving relationships in social life, they allow a fairly calm and serene growth, avoiding negative experiences that could be encountered by children or adolescents who have developed low self-esteem, such as drug use / abuse. Recent studies have shown that boys undergoing drug treatment for ADHD were at lower risk for substance abuse than were their ADHD peers not undergoing drug treatment. Furthermore, these studies highlighted how similar the percentages of substance abuse were found between boys without ADHD and boys with ADHD who had received drug treatment. We can conclude that abuse and addiction are practically non-existent in children treated even for long term with psychostimulants. In a very recent joint study by the University of Massachussets (Prof. Barkley) and Wisconsin (Prof. Fischer) published in Pediatrics of January 2003, carried out on 147 boys treated with methylphenidate and followed for 13 years until adulthood, all the other 11 previous studies carried out in this regard were confirmed and it was again concluded that "there is no consistent or convincing evidence that treatment with stimulants in childhood or adolescence is associated with the risk of substance abuse in adolescence and in adulthood, the greater frequency of such use in adulthood, or the greater likelihood of having a substance addiction or a real substance abuse disorder ".

Myth: Stimulant's "cover" the problem, without addressing the actual causes of ADHD.

Reality: The stimulants act in such a way as to improve the neurotransmission of dopamine and norepinephrine, neurotransmitters which are associated with very important functions of brain inhibition and modulation, in essence, the brakes of the brain. Their use does not differ much, for example, from the use of insulin for the treatment of diabetes. That is, it is a "replacement" therapy - even if the term for ADHD is not quite correct - but unfortunately, as with insulin, psychostimulants have only a temporary effect. It is this temporary effect that leads one to mistakenly believe that the psychostimulant masks the problem without solving it. At present they represent the only treatment that normalizes the inattentive, hyperactive and impulsive behavior of ADHD children. Among other things, this circumstance is also important because, as already pointed out above, if the child were to reach adulthood without adequate treatment, he could manifest all those psychic disharmonies or real psychoses, as a consequence of his own social failures and scholastics.

Myth: Stimulant drugs prevent growth.

Reality: Recent studies have shown that the adult weight and skeletal size are not affected by them taking stimulants and that the effects on weight are absolutely minimal, although still it is good practice to monitor the growth of the child during the first year of treatment.

Myth: Stimulants can damage the heart.

Reality: All publications show a high intra- and interindividual variability regarding the effects on the cardiovascular system induced by stimulants but without causing problems. Nonetheless, some parents raise doubts about the appropriateness of chronic therapies and some campaigns report deaths and suicides in connection with taking these drugs. All commonly used stimulant drugs have some effects on cardiac output and blood pressure, but mild, similar to what can trigger physiological conditions such as digestion or running, therefore perfectly tolerable in healthy subjects, effects which, moreover, tend to fade or disappear with the continuation of therapy, according to what was found in a study that lasted for almost two years (Zeiner P. Body growth and cardiovascular function after extended (1.75 years) treatment with methylphenidate in boys with attitude -deficit hyperactivity disorder . J Child Adolescent Psychopharmacology 5: 129-138, 1995). Regarding the anecdotal reports of cases of sudden death in children treated with stimulants, the only reports concern children treated with repeated therapeutic doses of desipramine and with a combination of clonidine-methylphenidate , the use of which is recommended in selected cases and for non- responders to stimulants and for which, therefore, ECG monitoring is indicated due to the possibility of a slowing of cardiac conduction, highlighted by the increase in the PR and QRS intervals or the appearance of arrhythmias and tachycardias. It is important to point out that these events have never been reported in subjects treated even long-term and exclusively with the drug of first choice which is methylphenidate (Ritalin).

Myth: The efforts of teachers towards the attention problems of children can produce improvements equal to or greater than those produced by drug treatment.

Reality: It would be very nice if it were true, but the recent scientific evidence (in particular the study MTA - Multimodal Study of Children with ADHD commissioned by the National Institute of Mental Health of the United States in which 579 children with ADHD between 7 and 9.9 years of age for fourteen months and comparing the effectiveness of four different treatments separately) tell us this is a myth. Especially in boys with pure ADHD, multimodal treatment (consisting of drug therapy together with the best cognitive-behavioral therapies) was not better than drug treatment alone and cognitive-behavioral therapy was much less effective than drug treatment alone. The conclusion is that teachers and therapists must continue to make every effort with the most advanced techniques of cognitive-behavioral therapy to help those with ADHD but equally they must also understand that if we do not intervene on the biological factors that underlie ADHD, one cannot hope for great improvements.

Myth: Parents and doctors are pushed to indicate drug therapy because they are heavily funded by pharmaceutical companies.

Reality: The associations of parents of children suffering from ADHD worldwide are non-profit associations and their activities of mutual aid and dissemination and promotion of knowledge are carried out first of all thanks to the voluntary commitment of the parents themselves. Secondly, the activities are self-financed through membership fees, the sale of books and videos produced by the same associations and partly also supported by donations from individuals but also from external organizations and among these also those of pharmaceutical companies.

But what is important to underline is the absolute independence of the work and of the positions taken by the associations and this evidently because of a personal, suffered and deeply aware involvement on very well-known and in-depth scientific and social issues concerning the problems of their same children. Obviously, any form of pressure on the part of anyone should be excluded, because parents are exclusively interested in the quality of life of their children which always has important repercussions on the entire family unit. For this reason, all parents' associations have important and fundamental contacts with the scientific world and in general with the world of research in order to be constantly updated and deepen the best and most recent advances in the field of multimodal therapy. Parents' associations therefore can only support all treatments that have proven effective in ADHD therapy, including drug treatment, obviously taking a stand against remedies that have proved ineffective and without scientific evidence.

Precisely because of this myth in recent years even lawsuits have been brought against an Association with a long tradition and great value such as CHADD (the largest American association of families with ADHD children and adults) and the American Psychiatric Association itself. In fact, these lawsuits were brought by the Church of Scientology and the CCHR (Citizens Commission for Human Rights - an international psychiatry surveillance organization founded by the Church of Scientology with the advice of American neurologist Fred Baughman) even though the same causes were all withdrawn or rejected. As rightly pointed out in the report by Prof. Jan Buitelar in the Strasbourg seminar entitled "Attention deficit disorders / hyperkinetic disorders: diagnosis and treatment with stimulants" of December 1999 (paragraph 3): "psychotropic drugs for depression or 'ADHD is somewhat of a hindrance to the Church of Scientology as this sect's primary economic interest is related to making people happier and healthier through other means.'

The ideas propagated by the Church of Scientology and its affiliations present in many parts of the world (mainly the Citizens Committee on Human Rights - CCHR Citizens Commission for Human Rights) through all the means of communication at their disposal and among these numerous Internet sites and brochures since the 1980s in the United States and subsequently in Europe, as noted by the European Commission, have represented and still represent "serious health risks for children, denying them adequate treatment".

THERAPEUTIC INTERVENTION

No therapeutic intervention treats attention disorder with hyperactivity, but specific behavioral techniques can be used to help the child improve their behavior. For this reason, it is essential that parents and teachers turn to specialists (psychologists of the developmental age, child neuropsychiatrists experienced in this disorder), in order to receive constant support and the teaching of appropriate strategies to help the child.

Therapeutic interventions must adapt to the individual characteristics of each individual child, to his attention span, to his motivational and self-esteem levels, always setting clear and realistic goals. It is also equally important to systematically and sustainably implement the therapeutic methods that are recommended by experts.

Generally, good results are found using cognitive-behavioral therapy, through which the child can learn certain techniques of managing his own behavior with particular attention to the ability to self-control and to the most adequate and conscious regulation of his emotions, especially negative ones. Children with ADHD are in fact deficient in the coordination and planning of cognitive and behavioral activities, in particular in the inhibition of executive functions (those, for example, that allow you to set goals by overcoming environmental distractions).

The objective pursued using these strategies is to improve the self-regulation of the child's behavior and his level of attention, also increasing his level of motivation and self-esteem. For this reason, it is useful to encourage and support the learning of social rules through the use of positive reinforcements, eliminating punitive and anxious attitudes on the part of the parent or teacher. In fact, we want to reach the recognition of the problem by the child and the planning and organization of his behavior in order to overcome the difficulties. In this way it will be possible to obtain, in addition to a lasting change in the attitude and behavior of the subject, also a positive response from his reference figures, in particular from parents and teachers.

The most popular techniques to use with a child with ADHD are:

- ***problem solving***, through which the child defines the problem; learns, thanks to the help of a parent or educator, to devise alternative solutions; to consider the consequences of the different alternatives and to complete the choice made by evaluating its effectiveness

- ***the technique of verbal self-instruction*** in which the subject learns by explaining aloud how to motivate a choice, to implement it and then to think internally these "steps" through an internal dialogue

- ***stress reduction techniques and biofeedback*** that induces a better self-control of the child's state of activation

- ***affective education*** through which the child learns to express his emotions, especially negative ones, and to understand what events are caused by them and learns to develop adequate ways to manage them.

These techniques are explained to be used in different areas of the child's life (family, school, social, etc.).

However, it should be pointed out that the results are not achieved immediately and parents and educators must learn to tolerate the mistakes that the child makes before finally learning these techniques. School and family must learn to work in a coordinated way, using the same approach and methodology, if they are to achieve lasting results.

Therapeutic interventions must also aim to pursue the improvement of the child's relations with his family and social environment through a more adequate management of his behavior and must also improve academic results through the teaching and use of a correct method of study. In this way the self-esteem of the subject can be strengthened.

In addition to a specific intervention on the child (learning behavior management techniques and teaching specific psychoeducational programs) it is necessary to implement support programs for parents in order to help them to adequately deal with the difficulties of their child.

PARENT TRAINING

The parent training allows parents of children with ADHD to learn strategies to reduce problematic behaviors and improve relational mode

In families of children with ADHD, the parent-child relationship is often difficult and sometimes dysfunctional.

Parent Training is a psychological journey where parents learn effective educational strategies to reduce problem behaviors of children with ADHD and improve relational mode, becoming active participants in the treatment of the disorder.

Parent Training is a psychological intervention that gives parents the tools to be used for effective behavior management of their children. The term Parent Training is an expression that suggests how this program focuses on enhancing parenting skills in the parent-child relationship. It is a space where parents can practice understanding their child's behavior and employing constructive attitudes and learn to structure an environment that favors the child's self-regulation, autonomy and reflexivity.

In particular, the primary objective is to provide functional behavioral strategies to help parents manage their child's behavior, but also their own behavior as an educating adult, in order to improve the educational and emotional quality in the relationship with their children. In fact, parents acquire new skills and relational educational styles, which are the basis of a parenting style oriented towards problem solving.

The Parent Training path was introduced in the late 1960s, starting from the work of Constance Hanf, a clinician interested in modifying aggressive, oppositional and deviant behaviors of children and young people. Hanf based her work on the importance of parental intervention, recognizing the family as a fundamental resource to be able to foster positive behaviors in the child. This intervention has been found to be very effective in the management of children and adolescents with behavioral disorders, especially Attention Deficit / Hyperactivity Disorder, also known as ADHD. In these cases, common sense and willpower are often not enough: in fact, it is necessary to be aware and adequately know the problems of one's child, in order to be able to put into practice effective behavioral strategies in order to achieve specific goals, reduce negative behaviors and increase positive ones. Parents who are more reflexive, organized and coherent in their requests and actions, allow their children to develop greater autonomy in finding alternatives of thought and behavior. This does not mean that families with children with ADHD must have an extremely rigid and rule-filled lifestyle, rather that it is useful and effective to create a structured environment that gives the child a space and time to reflect on what is happening.

The first Parent Training interventions with parents of children with ADHD date back to the early 1980s, in the light of research and studies that highlighted the conflicting nature of parent-child relationships and interactions in the case of a child with ADHD: especially in situations with many requests from parents, it has been seen that children with ADHD are less adherent and cooperative to the indications and rules imposed by their parents, or that they are for a shorter time, and show more oppositional and non-complacent attitudes than their peers.

Despite numerous studies on the subject, the clinicians who owe most to the development and use of this approach in the context of ADHD are Russel Barkley and Karen Wells and colleagues. Starting from Hanf's model, Barkley defined an intervention path specifically for parents of children with ADHD, consisting of 8 to 10 meetings with a specialized professional; Wells and colleagues instead developed a more extensive and intense Parent Training program of 27 meetings, with an intervention focused not only on parents, but also on the school environment.

With this in mind, the idea of a multimodal approach in the treatment of ADHD acquires more and more value and today it is the most effective intervention in the therapy of this disorder, which implies the involvement of the family, the school and the child itself, in a path that sees the combination of behavioral therapies, clinical-psychological interventions and drug therapies, based on the severity of the disorder.

How does parent training work?

The Parent Training program generally provides for the holding of 8-12 weekly meetings between parents of children and adolescents with ADHD with a specifically trained Trainer, in most cases a psychologist. The interval between one session and another is specially designed to give families space and time to implement the information, advice and strategies learned in the various meetings and reflect, in subsequent sessions, on the difficulties encountered and the results obtained. All meetings are aimed at gathering information regarding situations in which your child uses inappropriate behavior and preparing parents for change. To encourage better monitoring by the Trainer and to give participants an opportunity to put into practice and experiment with the strategies learned right away, the Trainer usually assigns the so-called homework, which are discussed at the beginning of each subsequent meeting to evaluate its effectiveness and problems.

Referring to Barkley's original Parent Training program, the stages and objectives of the path are listed below.

Step 1: Information and investigation of the disorder

The Trainer describes the specific characteristics of the disorder, illustrating its causes, course, possible risk behaviors, effective and ineffective treatments. Both the most common and best-known elements are dealt with in detail, such as impulsivity and inattention, and those of which parents are usually less aware, such as frustration, anger, shame, feeling 'different' or 'wrong'. This initial moment allows, in the first place, to inform parents correctly and comprehensively about the disorder and its nature, and to increase their awareness of it; second, greater cognition allows them to better understand the mood, emotions and behavior of their children.

Step 2: Understand the parent-child relationship

In this session, parents learn about the causes of their children's negative and disruptive behaviors and identify them within their family environment, sharing and discussing previously experienced episodes with the group. The Trainer instructs participants in the antecedent-behavior-consequence model, in order to recognize and identify the events potentially triggering negative behavior and explains the four factors involved in the development of problem behaviors in children: characteristics of the child, characteristics of the parents, stressful events in the family environment, parenting style.

Step 3: Enhance Positive Interactions

The task of the Trainer in this meeting is to convey to parents the importance of relating positively with their children, especially during the manifestation of negative behavior. They are involved and invited to discuss this competence, to practice and practice with the group, to share their experiences.

Step 4: Extend Positive Interactions and Increase Children's Complacency

In this phase, parents are urged to notice and highlight their children's positive behaviors when they find themselves in difficult situations, giving them immediate and consistent positive reinforcements. Strategies are then illustrated for giving commands and rules in the most effective way: making direct, short requests, with achievable and short-term objectives.

Step 5: Use a points or coin system at home

Parents learn the Token economy system, a rewards system that provides for reinforcing the child's appropriate behaviors, in order to encourage greater attendance in the future. Parents will be asked to draw up a list of rewards and reinforcers that can motivate the child, and a second list of those behaviors and rules they would like the child to abide by, which are given a score or tokens when enacted. The points or tokens earned will give the child the opportunity to reach the final prize. Token economy objectives and rewards can be shared and decided with your child, to make him feel more involved and responsible in this intervention.

Step 6: Include 'Sanctions'

When inappropriate behavior occurs, the Token economy provides for the use of penalties, which consist in subtracting previously earned points or tokens. At the beginning of the program, the parent shares with the child the behaviors that will cause him to lose points.

Step 7: Use Time Out

In the event that serious negative behaviors occur, parents are instructed in the Time out technique, which requires the child to retire for a few minutes (one for each year of age) in tranquility in a space that allows him to get away from the non-functional behavior committed, so as to process it and calm down. Before starting, parents discuss and agree with their child the reasons that trigger the Time out and the number of warnings that the parent will give to the child before using it. At the end of the time out, the child goes back to his own activity.

Step 8: Regulate behavior in public places

In this phase, parents learn to extend the program even outside the home environment, with some precautions to be applied based on the external context. The Trainer identifies together with the parents, who in turn will share with their child, the places where the child tends to manifest non-functional behaviors.

Step 9: Problematic behaviors in school and preparation at the end of the program

Parents learn to use the prize system also at school, with the support of constant feedback from the child's teachers regarding functional and non-functional behaviors previously shared with him. In order to achieve this goal, collaboration between parents and teachers is important, which requires periodic sharing of the problem behaviors highlighted and strategies to learn how to manage them in the best possible way.

Step 10: Follow-up

This is a control session at the end of the path, in which parents and Trainer discuss the changes obtained, any resistance still present and how to manage them.

Why take a Parent Training course

Taking care of children with ADHD can generate strong stressful situations in parents, which risk having repercussions on relationships within the family and, consequently, on the symptoms of the disorder itself. Families of children with ADHD are often characterized by less 'emotional warmth' and parents experience feelings of poor parental competence and poverty of effective educational strategies, which can lead to feelings such as guilt, frustration, anger.

An important aspect that emerges from multiple studies in this field is the positive correlation between functional relationships and educational coherence within the family and a less severe symptomatology of the disorder, greater social acceptance and greater social skills. The family is therefore a fundamental resource to draw on for the treatment of ADHD, based on this, Parent Training aims to modify those relationships that are dysfunctional, providing parents with useful tools that can bring out the educational potential that each of them possesses, but which they sometimes struggle to implement.

Finally, this path offers parents an opportunity to share and compare their experiences and emotions: a space in which they realize they are not alone, in which they discover new sides and ways of being for their children and rediscover others, to which they now look with new eyes.

HOMEWORK STRATEGY

ADHD children have a specific difficulty in organizing and managing complex tasks, which is why doing homework is a rather difficult challenge for them, because it means having to take into account a myriad of information at the same time, such as which subjects they have the day after, what tasks have been assigned to them, with what materials they have to make them and much more.

This chapter will give you some useful tips to help these children to face the time of homework with strategy and organization, trying to avoid wasting time and reducing your and the child's sense of frustration, increasing the perception of self-efficacy of both.

What's the use of homework? First of all, it is important to reflect on why it can be useful to do homework. Often both teachers and parents are focused more on the success of the task itself and less on the educational significance it can have. Doing homework, in fact, is an action that goes far beyond simply having "answered the questions well", it implies, in fact, being able to respect a commitment made and do it in an organized manner. It is an important challenge to be faced and faced and, alas, a complex challenge for those with organization and short-term memory problems.

Helping the child with ADHD to do his homework not only serves to get a good grade the next day, but it means "training" him to become more and more autonomous in completing a commitment or a need. Being autonomous can also mean understanding when it's time to ask for help, to admit "I can't do it,

I need support". We would not prevent a dyslexic child from using a speech synthesizer to do his Italian homework well, in the same way we cannot prevent the boy with attention and self-control difficulties from using organizational supports to complete his school tasks.

At this point, I invite you to stop for a moment and reflect on your idea of why it can be useful to do your homework. This is because, whether you are aware of it or not, your idea of why it is important (or not important) to do the homework also influences what you will do with the child you are trying to help.

STOP FOR A MOMENT AND TRY TO COMPLETE THIS SENTENCE:

IT IS IMPORTANT TO DO YOUR HOMEWORK

BECAUSE ....

Then ask the same question to the child you intend to support in carrying out the homework, using words similar to these:

"Mark, before starting homework today I would like to reflect with you on one aspect: in your opinion, what is the use of homework? Some children your age have answered this question in this way:

- I need to have good grades
- To learn something interesting
- To be satisfied with going to school
- To make mum and dad happy
- To avoid the sermons of mum and dad
- To have more time to play

- To feel that I have done my duty
- To train myself for daily commitment

What do you think about it?"

This reflection will help the child to rediscover his real motivation to do his homework. We are all willing to strive to change things around us and to learn new skills, if we are convinced that this can serve us some purpose, otherwise it is useless to talk about it and it is useless to think that we can make a change. In fact, if it were to come out that doing homework is important, but it costs me too much effort, it is the right time to catch the ball and ask the child: "Would you like to learn tricks, ways, to succeed better in this challenge?" before asking to him to commit himself in this sense.

Strategies and Tricks to study

For some children, doing homework can feel natural or even enjoyable, for many others, for most, it can become a nightmare. What is missing, very often, to succeed, beyond a real problem of fragility of self-control and attention, is knowing how to set up a series of strategic steps to follow. It is essential to immediately provide the child with a strategic approach with which to face the moment of homework, starting from asking himself where it is best to do them and how. Below I describe 3 central aspects in which it is useful to reason and decide even before "throwing yourself" into the mission tasks: the Where, the What and the How. Let's see them in detail.

What to do before starting: THE WHERE

Let's start by saying that the first thing to think about when approaching homework time, for a child or young person who has a fragility in the organization, is to prepare an adequate space. When I speak of space, I also mean the choice of the most suitable room, or the position in the classroom, in which the child has to do homework. It is essential that this is always the same and that it is not changed, but it is good to identify a room and also a part of the room in which to place the desk and make sure that the child always does his homework in that place. Similarly, in the classroom, it would be advisable to avoid having children rotate from one desk to another, but to guarantee the same type of spatial position, so that the child has fixed reference points.

The second aspect to take care of is making sure that the child puts on the desk, or on the desk where he usually does his homework, only the material he needs for the specific type of task he is about to do.

It may also be useful to establish an ideal space, for example an area of 2 mx 2m, around the table, in which the child can move freely: stand up, sit on the ground, etc. This means that he can begin to mediate between the need not to feel too "forced" and the rule of having to "stay in a specific space".

This aspect has an important educational and self-regulation purpose, as it somehow communicates the message "You have the right to do your homework as you want, you don't have to sit still and sit, but you still have to learn to regulate your behavior at inside a rule!"

An excellent point of meeting between what the environment expects and what he would instinctively do.

Things to do before starting: The WHAT

The second thing to do is to help the child ask himself "What should I do today? " This question will be easier to answer if you have already prepared a calendar of the week together, better if a clearly visible billboard attached near the desk, with written on the various tasks that are generally assigned for that specific day, such as the following:

For example, on Mondays I usually get my math homework for Friday; on Tuesdays I usually have my Italian homework to do for Thursday.

Things to do before starting: The HOW

At this point you will need to help the child identify steps to proceed with the tasks. One of the aspects that often discourages children (and even adults) is to view the tasks to be done as a vague and indefinite number of actions, being able to identify one step at a time can be much more encouraging for both.

A strategy that works a lot, especially with younger children, is to propose the steps to accomplish a task, such as the steps of a special plan to complete. It can be helpful to associate the idea of phases with the steps a superhero has to take.

A hero I often refer to when I work with the little ones is the special agent OSO, a cartoon in which a bear has to be able to carry out special missions and to do so he has to follow 3 phases.

I generally propose the following steps to the child:

✓ step 1: understand what to do;

✓ step 2: understand how I can do it

✓ step 3: do it

✓ step 4: check if I have done well.

The idea of carrying out phases, like a hero on a special mission, is very popular, motivating and "trains" the ability to tackle a problem in an orderly and strategic way, rather than to act by trial and error without a precise plan.

Tricks to stay alert

For the child with self-regulation deficiency, it is very tiring to remain attentive and concentrated, but also to decide to use strategies. To help him identify a number of strategies, I generally talk about "tricks" to maintain attention. In this chapter I take up some strategies suggested by Steer J. and Horstmann K) to help children with ADHD in school:

✓ Use stress relievers
✓ Move while standing still (we will see that there are exercises you can do to release hyperactivity and tension even when standing still)
✓ Make a phase plan

Let's see them in detail

Anti-stress

To release the tension, given by the frustration of having to do something out of duty, while he would like to do something else, you can suggest the child to use anti-stressors, such as anti-stress balls (which are ball filled with flour or rice.); or some rubber bands to snap, or even bracelets. A keychain with a carabiner, all this to give the boy the possibility to move while standing still!

Move, move… standing still!

Then there are some exercises that can be suggested and that allow the child to move while remaining in place. Some can also be made seated (for example at the desk, in the classroom or at the desk) and others require a minimum of space to move. Let's see them both.

<u>*a) Exercises to do while sitting:*</u>

• Lift yourself off the chair with your hands. You can tell the boy:

"This exercise is done like this: you have to put your hands on the sides of the chair, and push yourself down in order to lift your butt trying to take your feet off the ground."

• Press your palms together: "Place your palms against each other and push as hard as you can for at least 10 seconds and then repeat the exercise 5 times".

• Hands on your head: "You must sit up straight and interlace your hands on your head. You press down vigorously down for 5 seconds and then relax".

• Another way to relieve tension is to drink from a bottle with a sports cap like those of

Gatorade. This is because it requires you to suck with some effort, which allows you to release the tension.

b) Exercises to do with more space:

• Do a handstand on the wall: "Place your hands on the ground near the wall and throw your legs up into a handstand, keeping your head down. Place your feet on the wall keeping yourself straight and stay in position for 15/20 seconds. This allows you to release the tension for a moment and then maybe go back to doing your homework ".

• Wall Push-ups: "Lean against the wall with your hands and do push-ups while standing. Check that your hands are below your shoulders and that when you bend / straighten your arms your body remains rigid. Repeat 15 times "

• Table on the ground: sit on the ground: "Lean back by leaning back and lifting your waist upwards so that you have your hands and feet on the floor and your body and thighs straight just like you want to make a table. Stay in position for 15 seconds "

It can be useful to let the child / young person experiment with all the exercises and make him choose, from time to time, the ones he wants to do during the day's homework, so that he can feel that he is in control of the situation.

c) A strategic plan!

Putting together the PHASES method with the strategies to release tension, we could hypothesize, for example, the study of an English topic structured as follows:

- Step 1: I clear the table of anything I don't need and get out the English book
- Step 2: Fill the water bottle with a sports cap, like Gatorade, as I told you, and keep it to hand
- Step 3: I read pages 98-100 and, in the meantime, I use a stress ball because this is more tiring: stay focused while reading
- Step 4: I do 10 pushups on the chair, the first exercise of the "move while sitting" group
- Step 5: I do the exercises on page 100. If they are difficult in between I can do a few more exercises from the "move" sheet. For example, for each exercise I stop and do a handstand on the wall
- Step 6: You are done. Reward yourself by doing something you enjoy.

For example, playing wii, listening to music or calling a friend.

As the child completes the phase, he can mark it with an X on a billboard, or on a prepared sheet, and then move on to the next phase.

In summary, the suggestion is to assume a series of phases for each type of task that must be done, and when it may be appropriate to take breaks or use the antistress.

Be more organized

Disorganization is another typical aspect of children and young people with ADHD and it is a disruptive- specific aspect, this means that even in this the child struggles and fails not out of ill will, but because he is dealing with a typical deficit of the disorder. It is possible to help him become more organized by first working on motivation and then suggesting specific strategies that support him in the organization so that he knows how to use suitable supports where, due to his deficit, he cannot succeed on his own.

The first aspect you need to work on is definitely motivation, you could solicit a reflection on what would change in his life if he became more organized, asking, for example, questions like these: "what would happen for example at school, what would be better for school and why? " " What would be better at home and why?" " And what would be better with your friends?"

Once you have probed his motivation, you can move on to suggesting strategies. One of the problematic aspects that many parents report, for example, concerns the organization of school material, such as the preparation of the backpack. To the parents I usually follow, I propose this type of "Mission prepare the folder" associated with positive reinforcement. Here is an example:

A plan: prepare the folder

- Step 1: help the boy build a chart with a list of everything he needs for each subject.

- Step 2: invite the child to hang the timetable of the week on the wall (if he is in secondary school, he can copy it from the diary);

- Step 3: at the end of the day, and after finishing the tasks, reminds the boy to look at both the billboards: and tick off what he's done.

Conclusion

The fundamental aspect is to have a clear strategy in mind and translate it into concrete steps to be carried out with the child.

The goal is to help him become more and more autonomous in managing his small, and big responsibilities. Becoming autonomous does not mean knowing how to do everything alone, but it can and must above all mean knowing when it is essential to ask for concrete help and use support tools.

IEP OR LEARNING PLANS. YOUR CHILD IS ENTITLED TO SCHOOL!

Attention Deficit Hyperactivity Disorder is a neurological disorder that typically begins to show symptoms in childhood and progresses through adolescence and adulthood. More commonly known as ADHD, this particular disorder is characterized by excessive hyperactivity, difficulty concentrating or staying active, a perceived inability to listen or remain still for prolonged periods, and poor impulse control. Although these symptoms manifest themselves differently from child to child, they are almost universally destructive to a child's education, as a school environment requires skills in all of the above areas. Consequently, ADHD qualifies children for special resources and educational assistance.

ADHD is most commonly diagnosed in childhood, but it may not be diagnosed until later. If a child has not received a diagnosis before entering school, school can be instrumental in finding a suitable diagnosis for the child in question and can usually determine whether ADHD is a likely culprit for the difficulty in school based on behavior. of a child in a classroom setting. Although teachers cannot diagnose the condition, they can be a valuable resource in helping parents and children to obtain a legitimate medical diagnosis.

Students with ADHD are generally entitled to ADHD accommodations, including special education plans and altered learning environments. Some children with ADHD, for example, may be too distracted by background noise, such as a humming fan, window, or computer, and may need their teacher or teaching assistant to place them in a quieter area of the house or room. Others may find it difficult to focus on a single task for too long and may require lesson plans to be broken down into more manageable chunks of time or individual instruction from the teacher's assistant may be required. However, others may need additional sensory input and special permission may be granted to use a stirring toy or others distracted to focus on schoolwork.

These accommodations and more are decided through a meeting with a team of people from your child's school to formulate an individualized education plan or IEP. IEP meetings are usually attended by the teacher, therapists and school counselors, yourself and possibly your child. Usually, you also have the option to ask other people to participate with you, such as a therapist, primary care provider, or family member who is familiar with your child's unique needs.

IEPs are critical for children with ADHD, as they allow educators and parents to determine how a child is most likely to be successful in an educational setting and provide everyone with some peace of mind regarding a child's entry at school. IEPs have goals, in addition to education plans, and are reviewed as often as necessary. Sometimes, the goals are too difficult or goals have been achieved and new ones need to be created. An IEP meeting can be requested at any time, but need not be changed for 1-3 years after their setting, depending on a child's diagnosis and needs.

What do IEP meetings look like?

IEP and ADHD encounters are first called for children who have received a diagnosis. They can occur early in the year if a child has an ongoing diagnosis, or they can occur at any other point during the school year if a child receives a diagnosis in the middle of the semester, or if a teacher notices ongoing difficulty in the classroom. Fortunately, there are no restrictions on time-consuming IEP meetings during the semester, although they usually won't be called during the summer holidays unless a child is already enrolled in a summer school or similar program.

IEP meetings vary in time and complexity, based on educators and parents. If parents and educators are prepared in advance with desired goals, for example, and agree on a child's plan, an IEP meeting could be a short 15-minute effort. If goals are created during the meeting or if parents and educators disagree on ADHD goals or accommodations, IEP meetings can last a few hours and can even be spread over multiple sessions.

Parents and educators receive copies of a child's IEP and ADHD housing, so that they can both closely track a student's overall goals and progress, and any IOP-related concerns can be raised and changed throughout the year.

What to bring to your child's IEP?

IEP meetings can be unnerving at first; if you're not sure what to bring or what to expect, you may be taken by surprise. Bringing your child's medical and school records is a good start if possible. Notes of any additional therapies your child may be receiving are helpful, as you can work with your child's team of therapists and educators to create an integrated and seamless treatment plan.

Bringing a support system is also a good idea; you can bring another parent, family friend, therapist or lawyer to give you peace of mind as you work to create an ideal education plan for your child. This is especially true for controversial situations in which you and your child's educators do not see the eyes; While it's not necessarily a common occurrence, there is a possibility that your child's education team may not feel comfortable putting all the ideas you've come up with. In these cases, it is helpful to have a source of support, as well as a set of replacement plans, in case some of your ideas are not accepted or not possible in your child's school.

Any special systems installed at home can also be brought to your child's IEP meeting. Some children benefit from strict schedules at home, for example, consistent routines and reward systems. While teachers may not be able to implement everything equally, being able to recognize and provide effective motivational strategies for your child can help teachers develop similar techniques in the classroom.

Not all IEPs are created equal: educational pitfalls

Some IEP encounters go smoothly and all of a child's needs are considered, while others may be much more experimental, if a child has no previous goals or a child's education team is unfamiliar with ADHD and its unique challenges. Understand that IEPs, while powerful tools in a child with general ADHD education, do not guarantee a child's success and a child with ADHD may need more external support than an IEP can offer. Some schools, for example, may have more children with neurological and learning disorders and have fewer accommodations, while others may have fewer staff members and may not be able to offer frequent individual attention to your child. A child's school accommodation for ADHD is important but should not be confused with a health treatment or therapy plan for the child with ADHD; instead, work with your child's psychologist or primary care provider along with educational aids to create an ideal learning and development environment.

IEP for ADHD is very often the difference between a child who succeeds and one who falls behind in school; ADHD is a complicated condition and does not affect all children equally, so creating a specialized plan is critical in planning a student's success. Involving all those responsible for your child's care and development will ensure your child has as many different perspectives as possible, as well as ensuring that all of your bases are covered. An ADHD educator's perspective, for example, will differ from your pediatrician's perspective, as they see different aspects of the condition.

Ultimately, you are your child's best advocate. If you feel that the accommodations or changes offered to your child are not adequate, you have the right to request changes. If you feel that your child's teachers are reluctant or totally reluctant to abide by your child's IEP terms, you also have the right to demand that those terms are respected and enforced. ADHD is a difficult condition to live with, especially without adequate support. The support is far-reaching and can include people close to your child, such as you and other family members, understanding friends, and even a trained therapist, such as those found on BetterHelp.com, who is equipped to help you walk with you. and your child through the process of living with ADHD and getting help through the education system.

The incidence of ADHD is on the rise, and children with this condition require additional help to get the best out of school and beyond. Additional supports are readily implemented with the use of an IEP and can provide tremendous help to a child struggling with the ups and downs of ADHD. While it may seem intimidating or confusing at first, your child's IEP meeting is about having their needs met without fear of punishment or discrimination, so they can succeed and excel academically. If you are preparing to enter your first IEP meeting, or your 20th, staying calm and being prepared will ensure that your child gets the most out of his individualized plan.

Overview

If you have a child with attention deficit hyperactivity disorder (ADHD) who is having difficulty in school, they may need additional support. The Individuals with Disabilities Education Act (IDEA) and Section 504 of the Rehabilitation Act are two federal regulations to help students with special needs get the support they need.

According to IDEA, schools are required to develop an Individualized Education Plan (IEP) for eligible students with disabilities. An IEP is a specific plan designed to help students get the help they need. If your child has a condition that limits their ability to be successful in school but is not eligible for an IEP, they may be able to get support through Section 504.

Each school has a coordinator to ensure compliance with these federal regulations. If your child receives an IDEA or Section 504 designation, school staff will need to develop and follow a specialized education plan for them.

Obtaining a Section 504 or IEP designation

A specific procedure must be followed to obtain a Section 504 or IEP designation. Your child's disability status and support needs will determine their eligibility.

To start, your child's doctor will need to evaluate them. They will need to provide a verified diagnosis of ADHD. You will then need to work with your child's school to determine their eligibility and support needs.

Qualification for a specialized plan under Section 504

To qualify for a specialized plan under Section 504, your child must have a disability or impairment that "substantially" limits or reduces their ability to access classroom learning. Anyone can recommend your child to receive a Section 504 plan. However, your child's school district will decide if they are eligible.

There is no formal test to determine your child's eligibility. Instead, assessments are performed on a case-by-case basis. Some districts require a team of school staff with your help to determine your child's eligibility.

If your child is eligible, the school district will create a Section 504 plan for them. It will identify the accommodations your child needs, such as:

- frequent feedback from instructors
- behavioral interventions
- preferred seat assignment
- extended time to take tests or complete assignments
- possibility of taking the tests orally
- permission to record lectures
- peer assistance with note taking
- extra set of textbooks for home use
- computer-assisted education

- visual aids
- parental rights under Section 504

As a parent, under Section 504 you have the right to:

- receive notification of your child's Section 504 assessment and determination
- access relevant records relating to your child's Section 504 determination
- request a hearing on the actions of your child's school district regarding its assessment and determination
- file a complaint with your child's school district or the Office of Civil Rights

Qualification for an IEP under IDEA

If your child requires a more specialized or specific plan, they may require an IEP. They can also apply for an IEP if they need special educational services.

As a parent, you have the right to apply for an IEP for your child. With your help, a team of school staff will typically determine your child's eligibility and support needs. Your child will need to undergo tests and an evaluation. This may include tests for:

- intellectual ability
- academic performance
- vision disturbances
- hearing impairments
- behavioral impairments
- social impairments

- self-help skills

Most children with ADHD who qualify for an IEP also have learning difficulties or health conditions. If your child qualifies for an IEP, their team will develop a plan to meet their educational needs.

Parental rights under IDEA

As a parent, you have the right under IDEA to:

- receive notification of your child's IEP determination, assessment and placement
- access any relevant records relating to your child's determination or placement
- convene a meeting of your child's IEP team
- request a fair trial hearing
- be represented at meetings
- file a complaint with your child's school district or the Office of Civil Rights
- refuse to have your child evaluated or placed in a special education program

Take away

If your child has ADHD, they may need more support than their teachers, counselors, and school administrators are currently providing. If you think your child needs additional help, consider applying for a Section 504 or IDEA designation. School districts are required to comply with these federal regulations to help students with verified disabilities and impairments get the help they need. If your child receives a Section 504 or IDEA designation, school staff will develop a specialized plan or IEP. This plan will identify the accommodations your child needs. Getting additional support can help them succeed.

CREATE SCHOOL-FAMILY RELATIONSHIPS

The involvement of parents in the child's educational project is often decisive and of fundamental importance, in order to achieve the following objectives:

- ✓ Awareness of the disorder and associated difficulties
- ✓ Agreement on educational strategies, enhancement of the work done in the classroom, promotion of a containing context even at home

EDUCATIONAL CONTRACT

SCHOOL-FAMILY

Promote shared forms of school-family collaboration (eg fortnightly-monthly meetings, disciplinary "notes", diary, communication forms ...) that facilitate the child's participation in school activities and the carrying out of homework:

- Define 3 or 4 realistic goals, expressed in the affirmative
- Define times and methods for achieving the objectives
- Establish points and / or rewards for achieving goals
- Involve the child in the project aหd in the definition of the rewards

Clearly define the responsibilities of each:

- Teachers: fill in the form, assign points ...
- Parents: check the diary daily, assign rewards ...
- Pupil: fill in the diary, request the completion of the forms ...

EDUCATIONAL STRATEGIES

AND RELATIONAL EFFECTIVE - 1

• Review your vision of the problems manifested by the child with ADHD (eg listlessness, rudeness ...)

• Do not interpret problem behaviors as personal confrontations: they are part of the disorder

• Recognize the "diversity" of children with ADHD (eg difficulties, needs, needs of the specific moment ...)

• Revisit one's own relational modalities (eg rules, educational style, rewards and punishments, tone of voice ...)

• Reflect on one's relational style and on the behaviors that can trigger conflict situations (eg permissive or authoritarian attitude, excessive pressure, inconsistency ...)

EDUCATIONAL STRATEGIES

AND RELATIONAL EFFECTIVE - 2

• Explain pupils' problems to the class with

ADHD, the aids provided and the relational modalities to use:

• Only make promises that you can keep

• If something is not useful, do not do it (eg. Harass, lecture, argue, shout, offer easy "solutions", "be good" ...)

• Share decisions with colleagues to avoid manipulation by the child and promote educational coherence

• Do not correct the child for everything: evaluate from time to time on what to insist on and what to leave out

• Focus on core issues and overlook others

EDUCATIONAL STRATEGIES

AND RELATIONAL EFFECTIVE - 3

• Wait for the appropriate time to address problems

• Show empathy towards the pupil: make him feel understood and reassure him that he is not alone

• Keep Calm: Don't add any more stress to the situation

• Use a firm but calm tone of voice

• Resort to non-verbal corrections (eg gaze, physical stop, for example, sound prompts ...), avoid continuous explanations

• Orient the child in a positive direction before a problem occurs (eg avoid insisting, thinking about solutions rather than problems, doing a different activity ...)

Understanding of problematic behaviors: FUNCTIONAL ANALYSIS

• Problem behavior occurs in the presence of certain variables (causes) that trigger it:

- Unstructured situations

- Excessively complex requests

- Repetitive and / or prolonged activities

- Search for instant gratification

- Seeking the attention of others

- Avoidance of unpleasant and / or disturbing situations

• Understanding these causes helps prevent and / or anticipate problem behavior

DEVELOP THE AWARENESS OF PROBLEMS

• Develop the child's awareness of his difficulties, so that he can learn to self-regulate and prevent any problems (eg delays, damages, reproaches, discussions ...)

• Help the child anticipate the consequences of their actions

• Give frequent feedback on the correctness of the behavior

• Define precise deadlines to help the child manage their time

• Help the pupil to reflect on the reasons for the reactions of others and on what could have prompted these behaviors

• Reflect on the consequences of certain ways of speaking or behaving on others

Acting on the ENVIRONMENT

• Create an environment that is as peaceful, safe, structured and as routine as possible

• Prepare the pupil for changes in the environment

• Reduce sources of environmental stress (eg. Light, noise, temperature, confusion ...)

• Enrich or impoverish the environment

• Simplify the environment

• Limit the pupil's range of motion (eg dangerous situations)

The importance of the RULES - 1

• Children who have difficulty in self-regulating their behavior need to follow very specific rules that help them define what actions to take in various situations and what consequences, positive or negative, can derive from them

• The rules must be few and not too demanding for the child, otherwise there is a risk of generating oppositional behavior and it becomes difficult to enforce them, with negative consequences for the pupil and for the sense of effectiveness of the teachers

• Routines help the pupil to make the environment more predictable and thus to have more behavior

REGULATED AND CONTROLLED

The importance of the RULES - 2

• Define the rules in a simple, clear, concrete and positive way (eg "don't get up" vs "get up when you're done")

• Remember the rule or decision made by mutual agreement

• Anticipate negative reactions and reiterate the rule (eg. "I know this is tiring for you, but we agreed that ...")

• Establish rules and make sure that the pupil understands them and respects them: the child must know how far he can go

• Define rules that facilitate relationships (eg ask before taking things, don't make fun ...) and enforce them, to avoid the underlying feeling: "it's always me ..."

• Anticipating activities, problems, possible unforeseen events, punishments in case of non-compliance with decisions

POSITIVE and NEGATIVE REINFORCEMENTS

• POSITIVE REINFORCEMENTS = events that increase the probability of occurrence of a behavior (rewards):

- Material or symbolic (point systems)

- Social (praise, signs of affection, attention ...)

- Dynamic (pleasant activities)

• NEGATIVE REINFORCEMENTS = the behavior puts an end to an unpleasant situation (eg "if you finish this thing, then we won't do it anymore"). Be careful not to feed negative behaviors (eg. "If I have a tantrum, I get what I want")

TOKEN ECONOMY (operative learning)

• Use of point systems (stars, tokens, smileys…) that are given or taken away according to certain well-defined rules (eg wait your turn, stay in your seat, do not speak…). At the end of the lesson, day or week, the student can thus obtain a small prize, preferably chosen together with the child (more motivating).

• Effective behavior modification technique to give immediate feedback to the child regarding his behavior

PUNISHMENT

• Punishment = any consequence that reduces the likelihood of repeating the negative behavior

• The punishment can be implemented:

- By subjecting the child to a situation that is unpleasant for him

- Taking away pleasant things from the child (this category includes the following procedures: strategic ignoring, cost of response and time out)

• The punishment must be given without showing aggression, with the aim of educating the child and providing him with an adequate model of behavior, which he can adopt and imitate as an alternative to the negative one.

• Unjust or exaggerated punishments produce violent reactions of defense, rejection or withdrawal in oneself and demotivation

OBJECTIVES of the TECHNIQUES of REINFORCEMENT and PUNISHMENT

Encourage positive behaviors, demotivate problematic behaviors

• Define precise and feasible rules ("if ... then ..."):

"When your turn comes, you can talk" "If you sit down, you can draw"

• Give feedback to the child regarding his behavior

"Carl, you spoke without waiting your turn"

"Francesca, you answered without using the scheme we made"

• Valuing positive behaviors (positive reinforcement):

"Bravo, you answered in your turn!" "You did this job well"

STRATEGIC IGNORING

• Pretend not to hear or see the behaviors that the child engages in to attract the adult's attention (eg the child throws a tantrum to get attention or to continue an activity he likes).

• Initially this technique leads to an increase in such behaviors. Later, when the child realizes that he is no longer getting what he wants, he stops using that strategy.

FEEDBACK COST

In the face of negative behavior:

1. Propose behavior that is more appropriate to the situation (provide a model of behavior, understand the difficulty underlying the problematic behavior ...)

2. Give a warning (eg "if you push Andrea again, I'll take the game away ") Give the child the opportunity to behave appropriately and avoid punishment

3. Implement the punishment: loss of a privilege, a promised reward, or an enjoyable activity

TIME OUT

In the face of negative behavior:

1. Give a warning (eg "if you don't stop screaming, I'll make you go to your desk") Give the child the opportunity to behave appropriately and avoid punishment

2. Implement the punishment: make the child sit on a chair, quiet and calm, for a few minutes (2 to 5). If he stands up: Remind him that sitting is to calm him down and that he can go back to the previous activity, as long as he behaves appropriately. Tell him that if he continues to behave in this way, it will have a further negative consequence ("next time you will not do this activity again")

Alternative technique: remove the child from the situation

PROBLEM SOLVING

INTERPERSONAL - 1

Learn to hold back impulsive reactions and control your level of emotional arousal:

Sit down and calm down before speaking

Count to 5

Take 3 deep breaths (relaxation exercises)

Define precise rules of behavior (eg NO hands, YES mouth)

Use slogans (eg "think before you act")

Prepare cards / drawings suggestion:

1 CALM! Take it easy, breathe

2 Ask yourself: Why am I angry?

3 What happens if I do this?

4 Are there other ways to get along?

Motivate the child to self-control

PROBLEM SOLVING

INTERPERSONAL - 2

Define the problem in detail:

Understanding what is happening who, what, how, where, when, why

Identification in the situation

Identify the child's true goals: conscious goals may conflict with unconscious ones (e.g. being part of a group, developing a friendship, learning a new game vs attracting attention, taking revenge, winning at all costs, showing your superiority or get it right away ...)

PROBLEM SOLVING

INTERPERSONAL - 3

Learn to produce reasonable alternative solutions:

Help the child to change the goals that place him in a situation of relational conflict:

- While you are waiting for Andrea to finish drawing, what can you do?

- Tell me the name of another game you would love to play...

- Why do you think Andrea doesn't want to play with you?

- Why are you so sorry? Did you care so much?

- We can try to do this together ...

Reflect with the child on the consequences of his behavior (e.g. the teacher punishes me, nobody wants to play with me anymore, if I hurt someone then I feel sad ...)

Awareness of one's own emotional experience, mental flexibility, decentralization and empathy

PROBLEM SOLVING

INTERPERSONAL - 4

Implement the chosen solution:

Help the child in the implementation of the chosen solution (phases)

Provide concrete solutions or strategies to address difficulties

Monitor the progress achieved

Reinforce the positive result

Change strategy in case of failure

METHODOLOGY:

Establish a priori that childish or unrealistic solutions will not be taken into consideration

Avoid questioning the feasibility or rationality of a childish or inadequate response. Just comment: "Yes, sure, this is a possibility, but what other solutions could you think of?"

PERSEVERE!

• NEVER forget to recognize and value positive behaviors and qualities

• Whenever possible, trust the child, providing for moments of "control"

• Model for the child by showing how things are done

• Always start with something positive before negative

• Continue to help the pupil in areas where they show a deficit and a need for guidance and support

• When an intervention works, keep using it

• Be patient: it takes a long time to acquire the routines

HOW TO DEAL WITH A HYPERACTIVE CHILD AT HOME AND AT SCHOOL

School and family should forge a solid alliance, building a fruitful relationship aimed at avoiding the numerous frustrations that the child will inevitably encounter if you begin to storm him with reproaches and punishments, or having inadequate expectations of him, subjecting him to real "challenges" in which, he will be the loser (with further frustrations that reinforce the vicious circle).

Teachers should be aware that their different attitude towards the inattentive / hyperactive child has a strong impact on the modification of his / her behavior. In fact, it should not be forgotten that the severity and persistence of the symptoms of the disorder are greatly affected by environmental variables, how the child feels accepted and helped in the face of difficulties. One of the predictors of a better outcome of the disorder in adolescence lies precisely in the positive relationship that teachers have managed to establish with the pupil during the school years.

The "rules" of the class must be few, simple and understandable. The teacher, first of all, must act as an authoritative and competent point of reference and work alongside the child (without losing patience), giving him brief and simple instructions, specifying both verbally and in writing the most important steps to help him to properly perform a task.

Experience indicates that it is necessary to take frequent breaks during the lesson, making the work stimulating, firstly by involving the children as much as possible in "paths" in which everyone feels involved, and only secondarily, and gradually, by enforcing the times for carrying out the given task. It is absolutely counterproductive to underline, least of all sarcastically, the difficulties of the hyperactive subject, in order not to give rise to " labeling " even on the part of his companions, which would exacerbate the condition of explosiveness of the disturbed child.

Considering then that these children often lose their things, it will be useful to define the times and ways to achieve a routine reorganization of their materials. To this end, the use of positive reinforcements is important, to be varied with intelligence and sensitivity so that they do not lose effectiveness: one of these could be to favor the hyperactive child in the activities in which he succeeds best, avoiding - as mentioned - possible frustrating competitions with children.

Finally, when necessary, teachers, in addition to collaborating with parents, should discuss with experts to integrate and harmonize the interventions implemented on the child.

Hyperkinetic children: what to do

In the first place it is necessary that parents avoid blaming the child (or themselves) for behaviors that are not good and evaluate, instead, what are the occasions and moments in which it is appropriate to gratify the child. Aggressive or ironic behaviors towards the child arc also to be avoided, even if one often hears invoking "a healthy slap" in search of a bit of peace for these parents who are certainly put to the test. Requests addressed to the child must be clear, precise and coherent. If the adult is able to control himself, training himself to manage conflicts in a positive way, he will be able to constitute the facilitation that the child needs, that is, by example, he will provide the child with adequate strategies for solving various problems. On the other hand, as is well known, educating takes a long time: learning to communicate correctly is not easy and requires a lot of effort. In fact, often the same parents of "difficult" children find it necessary to follow a personal psycho- educational or therapeutic intervention, to learn about the child's difficulties, to relate to them in an evolutionary key and to enhance the child's positive behaviors.

Some principles of educational psychology to help the hyperactive child

The child must be accepted and understood for what he is. Don't send him negative statements, don't perceive him as totally wrong, and don't interpret any problematic behavior he has as a personal affront. This, in addition to being unproductive on a pedagogical level, also involves considerable stress for the adult;

Educate the child positively. It is important that educators point out even the smallest positive things he does, the least progress. Each of these actions must become an opportunity to gratify him, to show him that we are happy with his commitment;

Non-dangerous problem behaviors should be ignored. Behaviors of impulsiveness and restlessness should not be continually emphasized (unless they are dangerous for oneself or for others): on the contrary, inadequate behaviors often persist precisely because too much attention is paid to them;

Establish principles of behavior ("rules") and follow them (school plus family). In front of the children there can be no signs of disagreement or discussion, because such inconsistency would become a "breeding ground" for the restlessness of children;

The way of speaking to the child must be calm. When telling him what to do, be precise and use positive terms and expressions. Prohibitions and denials risk producing in the child first of all an emotional state of hostility or challenge and, moreover, they do not provide any information on what the child should do or how he should behave:

Do not scold the child in front of others, and do not tell his "feats" to other people in his presence. If he really needs to be reprimanded, it is better to take the child somewhere quiet and explain things to him calmly and firmly;

At school, as well as at home, it can be of great help to have a quiet work environment with a predictable and reassuring routine;

Offer a calm and thoughtful role model. The child must be able to understand how to deal with certain situations and how to solve them. In this sense it is very useful to verbalize all those arguments that we do internally to offer a behavioral model. The adult, speaking aloud, provides an example of reflexivity and a rational problem-solving strategy;

Promote the right amount of physical activity: team games are suitable (which teach to curb impulsiveness to encourage collaboration for a collective result) and sports that educate self-control.

Class organization can also help. We also discover the rules for the school.

It is advisable to check the sources of distraction within the class: it is not recommended to have the child sit near the window, the bin, other noisy classmates or very interesting objects. It is equally unproductive to place the student in an area completely devoid of stimulation, as he becomes more hyperactive because he searches for new and interesting situations.

Arrange the desks so that **the teacher can frequently pass between them,** to check that the most distracted have understood the task, are following the lesson and are doing the assigned work.

Shorten working times. Take short and frequent breaks especially during repetitive and boring tasks.

Make the lessons stimulating and full of novelty: hyperactive children with attention disorders perform worse when the tasks are boring and repetitive (using figures, patterns, often varying the tone of the voice, etc.).

Interact frequently, verbally and physically, with students.

Make sure they have to answer often during the lesson.

Use the name of the distracted learners to get their attention.

Build game situations to facilitate understanding of explanations.

Use role play to explain historical and social concepts in which various characters are involved.

Accustom the impulsive child to control their work. Even an order can help ...

It is also important to establish scheduled and routine activities, so that the child learns to predict what behaviors he should produce at certain times of the day.

It is important to clearly define the time needed to carry out the daily activities, respecting the times of the child (this also facilitates him / her to orient himself better over time). Helping the hyperactive learner to better manage their material, teaching them about organization and leaving them five minutes a day to order their things. The teacher must propose himself as a model, keeping his own material in order and showing some strategies to cope with situations of disorganization. Use the diary for effective daily communication with the family (not to write negative notes on the child's behavior, mortifying him).

How to handle a hyperactive child

First of all, it is advisable to define and maintain clear and simple rules within the class (it is important to obtain unanimous consensus on these rules).

Review and correct the class rules as the need arises.

Often it is necessary to clearly explain to inattentive / hyperactive pupils which behaviors are appropriate and which are inappropriate.

It is very important to make impulsive students understand what are the consequences of their positive behaviors and which ones deriving from negative actions.

It is more helpful to reinforce positive (established) behaviors rather than punish negative ones.

Emphasize the child's appropriate behaviors through broad and obvious gratifications.

Have the possibility, creatively, to change the reinforcements when they tend to lose effectiveness.

It is recommended not to punish the child by removing the interval, because the hyperactive child needs to release tension and socialize with his peers.

Severe punishments, written notes or suspensions, do not change the child's behavior, except for the worse.

It is important to set simple goals to be achieved on a daily or weekly basis.

It is useful to often inform the child about how he is working and how he is behaving (feedback), especially with respect to the objectives to be achieved.

Two things to avoid: do not create competitive situations when carrying out tasks with other companions and do not focus on the time of execution of the tasks, but on the quality of the work done (even if this can be lower than that of the companions).

And two things not to forget: it is necessary to use the strong points and to avoid the weak sides of the child as much as possible: for example, if he demonstrates fine motor difficulties, but has good language skills, it can be useful to favor oral expression, when it can be substituted for the written one. The second thing not to forget is that: we must emphasize the positive sides of the behavior such as creativity, affection, extroversion

OTHER STRATEGIES TO MANAGE THE HYPERACTIVE CHILD

In this chapter I will try to explain to you which is the best sequence of strategies to be able to effectively manage the behaviors of inattention hyperactivity, minimizing the effort and time of implementation. Pay them some attention and above all:

OPERA!

Observe

Projects

Run

Think

Adjust the shot

First: LOOK

"Stop, wait and you will save time, run, gasp and you will not arrive"

(Chinese proverb)

I know that you are in a hurry to respond immediately to the emergencies that often certain behaviors lead you to face and I also know that if you are a teacher, you have at least 20 other children in the class to manage in addition to the hyperactive child, while if you are a parent, you feel exhausted, perhaps frustrated or guilty because someone told you that your child's problems were your fault. I know all this and I know that for this very reason the idea of stopping to observe without intervening immediately makes you uncomfortable, because you have the feeling of wasting time and above all losing control of the situation.

In reality the opposite is true: the more you know how to stop and observe carefully, following a specific pattern I am about to tell you about, the more you will have clear what to do and you will save a lot of time and energy, rather than if you threw yourself into facing everything with any strategy not tailored to your child or student in particular.

Often when we are faced with a problem, the first thing that comes to us is to act immediately, do something, anything, just to try to reach a solution.

Precisely for this reason I have often heard teachers or parents tell me: "With him / her I have really tried everything: from sweetness to punishment, from indifference to rejection, to reward", and what I answer is that unfortunately, despite good intentions , this is precisely the problem, because having tried them all means only one thing: having given the child a series of conflicting information that has only increased his confusion and his need to seek coherence and structure that very often, as we will see soon, it translates into those problem behaviors that you are trying to avoid.

It is really important, however, to stop for a moment and observe before doing anything else. Observing, we need to understand, understanding we need to act in a targeted way and not to waste time and energy. The first aspect to become aware of is this: every child act and behaves in a context, so he often reacts to what happens in that context.

For many parents and teachers, it was enlightening to realize that of some problematic behaviors, it was possible to identify antecedent events that always occurred in the same way and equally recurrent consequences. For example: every time a new task is entrusted to him, Mark gets up from the desk and disturbs his classmates or asks to go out, the teacher punishes him, or every time he goes out for a walk, Luke insists that mum and dad buy him a game, he insists so much that in the end they give up and he immediately loses interest in the game he had so insistently requested.

In the first case, the antecedent is "the assignment of a new task" and consequently the result is "the teacher punishes him." In the second case, there is a recurring consequence that is "every time Luca makes a request insistently, the parents give in out of fatigue, implementing a communicative mechanism of the type" no, no, no, no, yes ", which unfortunately, only reinforces the behavior.

Identifying antecedents and consequences is extremely useful because if things always happen the same way, then we can predict them and above all we can do something about it!

An effective way to analyze antecedents and consequences of a behavior is to use the ABC form, a simple form that you start filling in from the second column (B) in which the target behavior is entered, and then move on to fill in the first column (A), in which everything that happens just before is inserted and finally, in column C, what usually happens after is inserted.

A

(Antecedent)

B.

(Behavior)

C.

(Consequences)

What happens before he / she does B?

What is the problematic behavior? Describe it in a concrete and observable way

What happens after he / she has done B?

TRY IT NOW! Take a piece of paper and copy the ABC sheet, try to think of at least 1 BEHAVIOR PROBLEM that occurs frequently and ask yourself: is there anything that happens just before he / she engages in that behavior, always the same way? And what usually happens next? A behavior always communicates something.

A very important thing to know is that a behavior does not happen without motivation, but generally expresses a need. And if the behavior is problematic, it usually occurs for 2 main reasons: to communicate something (request for attention, discomfort, other...) or to allow self-regulation (for example, releasing tension, filling a sense of boredom or emptiness).

So, after observing the behavior you have to ask yourself: what is the use of doing that? And if you have thoroughly analyzed the antecedents and consequences, it will be easy for you to answer this question.

If, for example, every time that mom gets up and leaves the room, Mark literally starts to dismantle the house, maybe he is dealing with a desire for attention / presence that maybe mom, who is understandably committed to something else, is not responding to, so in this case, Mark should be prevented from feeling disregarded because mum is leaving, perhaps involving him in what mum has to do or in another interesting task for him before her leaving the room.

Or if every time the teacher assigns a new task, Luke gets up and disturbs his classmates, perhaps the activated need is to regulate the emergence of a feeling of fatigue, since starting a new task requires an effort of attention and concentration. Here perhaps Luke is trying to regulate an emotion which could be prevented or favored by allowing him to help the teacher distribute the material for the task, eg.

Having this clear can help us no longer see the child as an uncontrollable Martian, but as a child who has a specific need that we can anticipate and gratify before it even emerges!

Try asking yourself if there are things you do or say before or after a certain behavior of the child that only reinforce the re-emergence of the behavior.

Very often what we do does not help us improve things. I'll give you an example: a teacher told me about a situation of this type: every time a classmate John got up and went to disturb the others, she punished him with a scolding and put him back in his place with force.

The punishment of the teacher, as she herself admitted, did not serve in the least to extinguish the behavior (in other cases the punishment, on the other hand, can be useful, but must be applied with specific criteria), on the contrary, it further irritated the child who promptly after a while got up again.

The punishment was likely to further frustrate what was likely his request (to be gratified and rewarded like his peers), triggering an unpleasant vicious circle.

In the example I gave you before, however, the one in which Luke insists on obtaining a game in which he then seems to lose interest when he got it, most likely, the game was not desired in itself. It was the reaction of interest (even negative attention) that the request aroused. Once he got the game, it lost its functionality and was therefore no longer interesting for the child.

What worked first of all, in these cases, was 1) Immediately stop the behavior that did not lead to the expected benefits (punishment or giving in to a request after repeated refusals); 2) try to understand what was the need that the child was expressing (for example, seeking gratification or interaction) and act in anticipation.

If when you react that way, the child continues with the unwanted behavior, why do you keep doing it? The first thing to do is to immediately stop doing what does not make you get what you want, you will save a lot of energy!

Most likely now you are asking yourself: "Yes, but if I stop doing what I have always done, what should I do then?" To answer this question, you must try to understand what the child's need may be. Do you remember what we said? A behavior always hides a motivation, most likely the child is expressing a request or a need for self-regulation.

TRY IT NOW! Go back to your ABC tab and start making some assumptions about the situation you've been thinking about: what could be the motivation behind what he does? Does he need to be praised? To self-regulate an emotion? To take a break?

Second: Design

If you have done what I have proposed so far, you are already well under way.

What you need to do now is decide how to act on the antecedents and consequences you have identified. The second step is to design a specific and targeted strategic plan to limit problem behavior as much as possible.

Remember that a good parent, like a good teacher, is not the one who knows how to stem the emergency, but the one who knows how to prevent it, because he has foreseen and anticipated what could happen and organized things so that it would not happen.

First of all, I remind you once again that: a behavior always expresses a need, for self-regulation or for recognition / attention, so the child is probably asking you something like:

"Recognize what I can do, let me feel that I am important and that I am fine as I am"

Or

"I need to take a break, because it is very tiring for me to commit myself like the others!" Or maybe it's expressing both.

So, at this point you have to reflect: if the need you have identified is a need for self-regulation, it may be useful to implement strategies such as creating routines and giving information, allowing moments to recharge, while if the need is to be gratified and recognized, it may be useful to act on the child's involvement and on a positive point reinforcement system.

I know what you are thinking: that the child probably shows both types of needs, well, then you can decide to implement even more strategies, but the important thing is to choose to start from one at a time! Below I will briefly describe them.

Create a routine and give Information

For each of us it is important to know what is going to happen to us, why we are where we are and what our role is at that moment, even for children. Especially for children who easily lose sight of a task and a goal, then we help the child to regulate himself by creating a routine and informing him of what awaits him.

Some teachers and parents have found a huge advantage in creating posters with pictures representing the activities that would be done in the classroom or at home during the day, scanned for half an hour, in the same way for others it was very useful to create cards or placards, which explained well in which place the games were stored, where the shoes etc. in practice they have fostered a mental order.

On the billboards next to each image there was an empty space and the child was asked to fill in the space with a cross as the activity was completed, or with stickers.

Similarly, you can create cards with the activities to be placed on the child's desk, or on the desk in his bedroom, then ask him to flip one card at a time as an activity is finished.

Allow to recharge the batteries

One way to help the child to self-regulate can be to allow him to move away from the activity / task he has been doing for a while or from the classroom for a few minutes, in order to release his tension and return to the more motivated task. Some teachers have found it helpful to give the child 4 cards with batteries drawn on them.

Children could "recharge their batteries" 4 times a day, recharging a battery meant being able to leave the classroom and take a ride outside and then come back after completing a task. After the break they leave the battery in a box with a battery charger drawn on it. Similarly, some parents have provided some "scheduled" break activities with a bonus card that can be used to play a favorite game or a run around the house.

This allowed them to be able to offload excess activity and also acted as a reward after completing a task. You can decide what the "battery charger" consists of, whether to go out, do a favorite activity, go for a run around school or home ...

Involve the child

A very effective strategy for channeling impulsive behaviors into functional actions is to involve the child by offering him / her assistant-teacher tasks.

You could start the lesson by starting with: "Mark, I need you: help me distribute these sheets to everyone" or "Mark, help me make sure that my classmates understand what the task is: listen to me carefully and repeat it to them (instead of saying: repeat me what I said, let's see if you understand) ", or, during the lesson"

Mark, help me check the progress of the work: take a tour of the desks and check how many have finished and how many have not".

At home you could say: "Mark, darling, I need you, help me set the table for breakfast, let's see how long it takes us today, let's try to beat yesterday's record!" Other tasks that can be given are: erasing the blackboard, writing what the teacher says on the blackboard, tidying up after a job, putting back clothes or games, even if only partially, and then being able to do a favorite activity immediately afterwards and everything you think can be delegated to a child.

These strategies allow you to achieve two objectives: they respond to a need for recognition (the child feels important) and they allow the channelling of the child's impulsiveness into useful and concrete actions.

Bonus with a points system

We have learned all the behaviors that we implement. A lot of what I am and what you are is the result of conditioning, positive or negative reinforcement.

It is true that there is an innate basis from which each individual starts to build his personality, as it is true that there may be aspects of a biological or hereditary nature that affect us, but this determines only a minimal percentage of what we will then be, a large part of the individuals we are is due to the environment and learning.

This is good news, because it means that we can continually learn new and more adaptive behaviors and we can decide to "unlearn" the ones we don't like, but how? Generally, we are led to continue to implement those behaviors that the environment reinforces in us, that is, that are rewarded and to eliminate those that are frustrated or little appreciated.

This means that if we want to favor a new behavior, we have to reinforce it a lot, especially at the beginning of learning, rewarding it every time it occurs. Very often I hear people say "But I assure you it's not doing anything good! It's difficult to gratify him! " I generally reply that it is not possible! Unfortunately, we are often the victim of a "halo" effect, so if a child tires us out because it is problematic, we tend to see everything he does negatively.

Well, we must strive to grasp even the slightest positive behavior and reinforce it immediately! "Well Mark, I see that you have listened to me looking into my eyes at this moment, I am very happy with you!"

It may be useful to structure a real points system, in which you inform the child that he will receive a point (which can then be spent on stickers, sweets, leaving the classroom, more...) every time he puts in place the desired behavior.

Remember that: initially the behavior must be rewarded EVERY TIME it occurs, then as it is emitted more frequently it can be rewarded by alternating (once yes and once no), then every 3 times and so on.

Also remember that: for a hyperactive child to be rewarded at the end of the day is too late, because his perception of time is faster, so the effective reward is immediately after the desired behavior has occurred.

Which of these tips do you think is best suited to the behavior you want to change? Choose one and plan immediately when and how you could make it, at least make a first guess then you can fix it later.

Third: Run

"I hear and forget. I see and remember. I
do and understand" (Chinese proverb)

Have you decided what you want to start with? Well, do it now! Within a maximum of 1 week try to implement the suggestion you have chosen, do not delay, otherwise you risk losing the motivation to do it. Give yourself deadlines, for example: first 3 days: I observe the child having the ABC card in mind, paying attention to note if there are recurring antecedent and consequent events of a certain behavior and I try to understand what kind of need expresses the problem behavior and with which strategy I want to face it.

In another 3 days, I carefully plan the intervention, prepare the materials, involve the child in choosing the rules and build the tokens with him, then I begin to implement the procedures.

One thing not to forget is that children need to be involved in drafting rules, building placards or reminder cards. Above all they need to be involved in identifying desired behaviors if you want them to be motivated to apply them.

We can involve them by asking them: "Children, how would you like your classmates to behave during the activities?", Or "Luke, to do this activity well we have to have rules, like rules of a game, what could be the rules that we need to do it well?" Then you can create a billboard of the main behaviors to be respected which must always be formulated positively and must not be many, respecting everything is like not having to respect anything, it discourages because it is too tiring and unrealistic. Some behaviors to reinforce can be:

In the classroom

Raise your hand before speaking

·Wait until the other has finished speaking before you have your say

·Listen by looking in the eye

·Stay in your seat and wait for the teacher to tell you that you can get up

Instead of saying: Don't talk, don't get up….

At home:

Make requests in a low voice

Stay still while you play

Put the toys back in the basket after using them

Play on the carpet instead of on the sofas

If you are angry, stomp your feet on the ground instead of hitting

It's very useful to associate the rule with an image.

Initially you have to make an effort to grasp even the slightest positive behavior and immediately reinforce it "Very well, Mark, I see that you are speaking in an appropriate tone of voice, I will give you a star immediately", or "in class we have found several important rules, you agree that they become the class rules?

Then I suggest a game: every time you manage to respect them you will earn a token! For example, now I see that you are all listening to me: a token to everyone!"

While it is important for us adults when others appreciate what we do and when they realize the effort, we put into achieving a result, for children being rewarded is at least 100 times more important, because their personality is not yet definitively structured and therefore, they have not yet "decided" in a definitive way within themselves whether it is worth believing in themselves, whether they are smart people or not.

As parents and educators, we have a duty to build in this sense, to add a few more bricks every day to build their self-esteem. With ADHD children, in particular, we must remember that because of their disorder, they find it much more difficult than others to pay attention or to stay still, so they should be rewarded even more when they succeed even for a very short time, in what for them is difficult.

TRY IT NOW! Calendar in hand, decide now when you will start observing, when to prepare the materials, when to apply the chosen strategy!

Fourth: Think

In a 2000 article entitled the "progressive portfolio of skills" Michele Pellerey, a great pedagogist, wrote: "at the basis of the acquisition of skills is the ability to reflect adfore, during and after an action".

Basically, it means that we become competent in a new behavior if we reflect on how we are doing it, what works and what doesn't. Always remember to stop for a moment, before doing something, during and after. First asking yourself: what am I going to do, what do I want to achieve and how will I do it, while stopping from time to time to ask yourself: how is it going? What's working and what's not? What can I change? And afterwards ask yourself: how did it go? What worked? What would I do different next time? If you want let me have your thoughts! A useful form for self-observation can be the following:

Self-observation sheet

1. How did I feel in realizing what I had proposed?

2. What did I like /not like in what I did?

3. How did my child / pupil respond?

4. What aspect of the implementation worked?

5. What aspect of the implementation did not work?

6. What were the strengths?

7. What were the weaknesses?

8. What would I change in applying this strategy / activity next time?

TRY IT NOW! After having implemented the strategy, you have chosen, remember to fill in the self-observation form, reflecting on your work is a fundamental aspect of any new learning.

Fifth: Adjust the shot but ... in small steps ...

If you have observed yourself carefully, you will also have been able to identify the points to improve in your application.

The secret of a good educator, parent or teacher, is that he is always researching, that is, he never tires of making hypotheses, checking them and adjusting his aim, he acts and reflects on how it went, and then tries again starting from what he learned from his previous experience.

Above all, he is not discouraged by the first difficulties, he knows that to obtain good results it takes commitment, but also strategy. If you apply the steps, I have suggested carefully, the results will not be long in coming.

All gradually…. There are probably at least a couple of tips that you would like to implement right away, but I recommend starting one at a time, so that you can design and implement it with care. Do not be in a hurry, set yourself an achievable goal by adapting the examples I have proposed to you to your specific situation, trust above all in the fact that you can certainly create even better adaptations than those I have proposed to you because they will be "tailor-made" to your specific situation.

Practical advice

1

Identify the reason for their hyperactivity. Keep track of when they are hyperactive, and the events that preceded their behavior. More information will allow you to prevent symptoms or take action to calm them down. If they become hyperactive by eating certain foods, do not overdo the amounts.

2

Speak in a calm voice that doesn't let your emotions leak out. You will help them calm down and you will be perceived as having the greatest level of power over the situation.

3

Give them your attention. Often hyperactive children simply demonstrate a request for attention, and only for this reason they manifest symptoms of hyperactivity.

4

Don't lower their self-esteem by challenging them, always choose the path of kindness and ask them to stop.

5

Try giving them physical relief. This could be a massage or access to a stress ball.

6

Let them vent their energies. For example, allow them to run and exercise.

7

Challenge their goals to reconsider their behavior.

Sometimes children are hyperactive because they enjoy annoying us, knowing that this is not what we want. React to their call for attention by using reverse psychology to dissuade them from their harassing actions. If they lose the purpose of their behavior, they will not have an incentive to continue it.

SELF-CONTROL TECHNIQUES

Teaching self-control techniques to hyperactive children is one of the greatest gifts we can give them. In fact, self-control is one of the most important skills in life and a predictor of the success we may have in the future. This was demonstrated by a classic psychology experiment developed in the late 1960s at Stanford University.

The experiment that demonstrated the importance of self-control in children.

Walter Mischel recruited 4-year-old children to carry out his experiment. When the children entered the room, they found a table on which there were cakes and a bell. The psychologist told them that he had to leave the room for a few minutes, and that if they could resist the temptation and not eat the cakes, when he returned, he would give him two cakes instead of one. He also told him that they could ring the bell to call him, but in that case, they could only eat the dessert that was on the table. In practice, the children realized that if they waited patiently and repressed their impulses, the reward would be greater.

As expected, one third of the children decided to eat the dessert immediately and another third waited a while before ringing the bell. However, there was a group of children who patiently waited for the highest reward.

Ten years later, this psychologist contacted the parents of the children who participated in the experiment. He discovered that the children with the greatest self-control had become independent adolescents, with intrinsic motivation, able to cope well with difficulties and failures. Conversely, children who quickly succumbed to their impulses became adolescents less tolerant of frustration, more disorganized, and with a predominantly extrinsic motivation.

These findings, which have since been replicated in other experiments, suggest that self-control is formed at an early age and is a cornerstone of personality and how to react to life's challenges. The good news is that there are several self-control techniques for hyperactive children, so that they can learn to control their impulses and manage their emotions from an early age.

3 FUNDAMENTAL COMPONENTS OF SELF-CONTROL

First of all, it is essential to understand that self-control is the ability to regulate emotions, thoughts and behaviors in the face of temptations and impulses. It is an executive function that helps us adjust our first responses to achieve other goals or better adapt our behavior to the environment.

However, self-control is a complex skill in which other skills are involved:

1. **Introspection.** To exercise self-control, you must first be able to recognize emotional states and stop before reaching the point of no return. This means that it is essential to develop the capacity for self-observation or introspection.

2. **Impulse blocking**. Later you need to block the impulses, so that you can think of a better response. The ability to block instinctive reactions does not develop fully until the age of 7, when the prefrontal lobes are mature enough, but it can be stimulated even at an early age.

3. **Self-reinforcement**. Finally, it is important to understand that self-control is not an inexhaustible capacity, it must go hand in hand with the capacity for self-motivation. It means that the child should feel satisfied with his results, he must feel that he is moving in the right direction, for which it is necessary to reward him and congratulate him on his successes.

Techniques for developing introspection and the ability to block impulses

1. Game of statues

It is a fun and very effective technique for developing self-control in younger children. It consists in the fact that the child remains motionless when he hears the word "statue". To further complicate the game, we can include grimacing or weird movements to try to make the child laugh.

The goal of this technique is for the child to learn to control his impulses, thus stimulating the development of the prefrontal areas of the brain, which do not finish maturing until about 7 years of age.

2. Weather forecast

The goal of this technique is to promote the child's emotional awareness, making him develop introspection. In the beginning he will have to be guided, so it is important to sit next to him and ask him how he is feeling at the moment. He can be asked: "What's the weather in there?"

If he is feeling relaxed and calm, he can say that the sun is shining, if he is worried, he can say that there are clouds and if he is feeling very tense, it is about to start raining. The idea of this technique is that you observe the "time" that is going on inside him but without getting attached to those moods.

This way he will learn to quickly spot the signs of anger and anger, increasing his emotional awareness.

3. The volcano

It is a very effective self-control technique for hyperactive children, especially in those moments when the child seems about to explode. The idea is to make him use his imagination to make him aware of his behavior, so that he can sense when he is about to behave improperly and stop before reaching the point of no return.

We ask him to imagine his interior as if it were a volcano, which contains all his strength and energy. It must be explained to him that, like all volcanoes, even his inner volcano sometimes loses control and erupts, causing his emotions to explode. This way he will learn to distinguish anger, anger, irritability or frustration.

4. Touch water or sand

It is a holistic self-control technique that uses sensory stimuli, perfect for children who calm down through the senses. It is only necessary to find the most relaxing stimuli for each of them.

Some may calm down playing with water, adding a little soap for foam or bubbles. Others relax by playing with sand. The key is that more sensitive children have a lot of fun with different materials and aromas, so that they can be used to calm their emotions.

5. Soap bubbles

This infantile self-control technique pursues the goal of achieving calm by regulating breathing. But since it is difficult for young children to practice diaphragmatic breathing techniques designed for adults, this is a fun version suitable for them.

It consists of imagining making bubbles, for which the child will have to control his own breathing. It will have to blow softly so that the bubbles form. At first, we can accompany him and show him how to do it.

The interesting thing is that through the control of breathing it is possible to balance many other functions of the organism, such as the heart rhythm, which is why little by little anger and anxiety disappear.

6. The frog

The goal of this technique is to make the child understand how to learn to breathe deeply and give a positive outlet to emotional states. He is told that he can imitate a frog, an animal capable of making great leaps, but also of remaining very calm, observing what is happening around him without reacting immediately. He is then asked to breathe like a frog, slowly, inhaling the air through his nose while inflating his belly and releasing it very gently through his mouth as he deflates. As he breathes like the frog, many thoughts can appear in his mind, we teach him to notice them and let them go, while he focuses only on the breath and belly movement.

7. The anti-stress ball

This adult self-control technique also works for children. In fact, we can help them build their own stress ball, which is simple and fun.

You need to have a thick balloon, or put one inside the other to make it more resistant and fill it with rice or sand. It is important that the ball is not too big because it must fit in the palm of the child's hand. Later he can also paint a face on it or customize it as he prefers.

Then, when he feels tense, anxious, frustrated, or irritated, he'll just have to pick up the stress ball and play with it.

8. The jar of calm

This technique should be part of any parent's arsenal of educational resources as it works the same way as yoga, meditation or relaxation, helping to clear the mind. The secret lies in the fact that the movements of the colours inside the bottle have an almost hypnotic effect that captures the attention and helps the child to clear the mind of all those thoughts that fuel anger or anxiety.

To prepare the jar of calm you have to fill a transparent plastic bottle halfway with hot water and then add a little transparent liquid glue and glycerin, the glue will make the water thicker, so the more you put it the slower it will be the movement of the small grains. Then add a little more water, leaving a finger of air so that the contents have enough space to move. When the child needs it, he can shake the jar of calm and relax.

9. The traffic light

It is a self-control technique for hyperactive children to learn to regulate their impulsive behaviors and outbursts of anger. To apply it, the hyperactive child must learn to identify the signs that indicate that he is angry or irritated. When he perceives them, he has to "act" as if it were a traffic light.

Red indicates that it must stop; that is, remain quiet until he calms down. Yellow indicates that he has to think about what is going on and look for more assertive solutions. Green indicates that it can take action to implement the solutions.

At the beginning it is advisable to accompany the child, teaching him to identify the signs of anger or irritation and apply the colors of the traffic light together with him.

10. The wheel of possibilities

It is a self-control technique that consists of creating a wheel together with the child that represents a list of possible activities that he can do to calm down when he is feeling angry or frustrated. The wheel will have the shape of a cake and will be drawn on cardboard, where small spaces will be drawn in which the activities are written or, if the child is very young, he is asked to draw or paste photos that represent them.

Some examples of alternative activities to anger can be: drawing, counting to ten, jumping, listening to his favorite music ... Any activity that helps him relax is fine, as long as it does not compromise the integrity of the child or those around him.

It is important that the child makes an effort to propose activities that relax him. Then, when he gets frustrated or angry, he just has to turn the wheel of possibilities and do the corresponding activity. And finally, it is advisable to avoid being a helicopter parent if you don't want to have hyperactive children.

www.ingramcontent.com/pod-product-compliance
Lightning Source LLC
Chambersburg PA
CBHW071523150726
48000CB00002B/651